BASIC ANTHROPOLOGY UNITS

GENERAL EDITORS
George and Louise Spindler
STANFORD UNIVERSITY

COMMUNITARIAN SOCIETIES

JOHN A. HOSTETLER

Temple University
with the assistance of
ERIC MICHAELS
and
DIANE LEVY MILLER

Communitarian Societies

HOLT, RINEHART AND WINSTON, INC.
New York   Chicago   San Francisco   Atlanta
Dallas   Montreal   Toronto   London   Sydney

Library of Congress Cataloging in Publication Data

Hostetler, John Andrew
Communitarian societies.

(Basic anthropology units)
Bibliography: p. 58
1. Collective settlements—United States.
2.   Oneida Community.   3.   Bruderhof Communities—
History.   I.   Michaels, Eric, joint author.
II.   Miller, Diane Levy, joint author.   III.   Title.
HX654.H59   335'.9'73   73–19897

ISBN: 0–03–091291–1

Foreword

THE BASIC ANTHROPOLOGY UNITS

Basic Anthropology Units are designed to introduce students to essential topics in the contemporary study of man. In combination they have greater depth and scope than any single textbook. They may also be assigned selectively to cover topics relevant to the particular profile of a given course, or they may be utilized separately as authoritative guides to significant aspects of anthropology.

Many of the Basic Anthropology Units serve as the point of intellectual departure from which to draw on the Case Studies in Cultural Anthropology and Case Studies in Education and Culture. This integration is designed to enable instructors to utilize these easily available materials for their instructional purposes. The combination introduces flexibility and innovation in teaching and avoids the constraints imposed by the encyclopedic textbook. To this end, selected Case Studies have been annotated in each unit. Questions and exercises have also been provided as suggestive leads for instructors and students toward productive engagements with ideas and data in other sources as well as the Case Studies.

This series was planned over a period of several years by a number of anthropologists, some of whom are authors of the separate Basic Units. The completed series will include units representing all the basic sectors of contemporary anthropology, including archeology, biological anthropology, and linguistics, as well as the various subfields of social and cultural anthropology.

THE AUTHOR

John A. Hostetler is Professor of Sociology and Anthropology at Temple University in Philadelphia, Pennsylvania. He began teaching a course entitled "Communal Societies" before the dawn of the modern communal movement. His interests lie in cultural anthropology, specifically in both traditional and modern communitarian societies and their socialization practices. His publications include *Hutterite Society, Amish Society, Children in Amish Society,* and *The Hutterites in North America.* The last two titles were co-authored with anthropologist Gertrude Enders Huntington, who served as principal fieldworker in the research projects. His studies were cited in the United States Supreme Court decision (*Wisconsin* v. *Yoder,* May 15, 1972) that restrained the states from compelling Amish children to attend high school on completing the elementary grades.

Invaluable assistance was also provided by Eric Michaels and Diane Levy Miller, students at Temple University when this book was written. As students in John

Hostetler's course in communal societies, each wrote a preliminary draft of a chapter in this volume. Mr. Michaels wrote of his experience as a member of the Family commune, reconstructing from memory the essential characteristics of the group. He also contributed insights to the final chapter. Mrs. Miller assisted in the research and wrote the original draft of the chapter on Oneida.

THIS UNIT

Possibly no other movement in contemporary American society has elicited as much interest, enthusiasm, and antagonism as the movement to communes and related social groups, which has accelerated so markedly during the last decade. That communes and communitarian societies are a response to the perceived lack of morality and humanity of modern society, as well as to self-loss and feelings of alienation, is news to no one who has been watching young people recently. But, as John Hostetler points out, the search for alternative life styles is not new. Some of the experiments conducted as a part of this search have proved successful. After a few short years or even months, however, the vast majority have disappeared, though perhaps not always failing in the strict sense of the word.

John Hostetler gives us a brief historical background for understanding the communitarian tradition in American society and then indicates how the approach of anthropology can bring some insights to our understanding of this phenomenon. To give us a sample of distinctive communal groups from different time periods and ideological perspectives, he selects three: the Family, a contemporary commune founded in the late 1960s; the Oneida Community, formed in the New England states during the nineteenth century and still existing as a joint-stock company; and the Hutterites, who originated in the Austrian Tyrol and Moravia during the Protestant Reformation in the sixteenth century. The Hutterites have survived well and today are a thriving and expanding population of more than 22,000. The other two have been more short-lived but even so outlast by years the vast majority of experiments that fall somewhere within the range established by these three selected types of communitarian societies.

Though the history of each of these three groups is summarily included, the approach to their study is ethnographic. The goal is to describe the people and their behavior from the viewpoint of the trained ethnographer and to discover, as well, how the people view themselves. The description focuses on core concepts, including origin, ideology, subsistence behavior, social patterns, and polity. The Family and the Hutterites could be studied in the manner most familiar to readers of anthropology, that is, through participant observation. Eric Michaels, a former member of the Family, reconstructs from memory its major features. Author Hostetler has been a long-term participant-observer with the Hutterites and the Old Order Amish and has published extensively on both with his co-worker, Gertrude Enders Huntington. Oneida had to be approached differently, since it has not existed as a communitarian society since 1880. Through research into existing descriptive sources, the author and Diane Levy Miller were able to arrange the material within the same essentially ethnographic framework as the other two sections.

As aids to further study of communitarian societies, a selected reading list, questions for study and discussion, Case Study interactions suggesting comparative analyses, and a list of relevant Case Studies are provided at the end of this unit.

George and Louise Spindler
General Editors
STANFORD, CALIF.

Contents

COMMUNITARIAN SOCIETIES

Introduction
to Communal Types

"Community," "brotherhood," "communal experiments," and "utopian movements" are familiar phrases used to describe a rapidly growing phenomenon in the modern world. The number of communes and their variety, from highly idealistic experiments to student "crash pads," defy any reliable statistics. Apparently originating at least in part in science fiction, the growth of the communitarian movement has evolved far beyond fantasy. Contributing factors have included widespread alienation and the loss of personal identity, for whole segments of the modern population can no longer locate themselves individually or socially, nor realize themselves adequately in the atmosphere of modern society.

The search for alternative life styles is not really new. Throughout recorded history there have been periods when people sought to exchange the tyranny of property, social hierarchy, and archaic institutions for more humane ways to live and to share their possessions. Some of the past efforts to establish communes proved to be failures. Others, however, through the passage of decades and centuries, have been innovative in the sense of creating alternative social structures. Some social experiments following the Reformation, for example, solidified into sectarian, closed communities that have survived for centuries.

Before further discussion of the communal movement's background, two key concepts must be clarified—"utopian" and "communitarian."

UTOPIAN SOCIETY

Utopian thought has been a persistent theme in the recorded history of man. Robert Owen of England came to the United States in 1825 "to introduce an entirely new system of society; to change it from an ignorant, selfish system to an enlightened social system which shall gradually unite all individuals into one and remove all causes for contest between individuals" (Holloway 1966:104). By appealing to the ideals of socialism, Owen worked ardently to build New Harmony in Indiana. At the end of one year there were a thousand members. After eighteen months the new system had collapsed, for however good his dreams, plans, and writings, the new system did not work in practice.

The utopian leader attempts to create a new social order that may in time become universally accepted. He cares not only for immediate modifications, but yearns for universal improvements—for a new culture cleansed of injustice and pain. He prefers to reform the world rather than to resign from it.

It is the idealist, the reformer, who institutes the utopian society, founded on the proposition that man is a rational, willful, conscious, and intentful actor. These believers are optimistic about the nature of man, stressing that man has the potential for goodness, which is attainable if he is placed in the proper society. If nourished in the proper social context man will emerge as a noble product. Coming about only through optimal human will and effort, utopias stand in contrast to millenarian societies, which appeal to supernatural or catastrophic intervention (Tyler 1944:68–85).

Utopianism represents a tradition of thought about the perfect society and about the reoccuring dream of stability in which perfection is defined as harmony. "The harmony is of each man with himself and each man with all others" (Kateb 1968:267). Some writers (students of society) have characterized utopias as uniform societies where there exists universal consensus on prevailing values and institutional arrangements, implying an absence of conflict. There is no place in utopia for revolutions, riots, strikes, or poverty. Although frequently caste societies, they are such by willful consent and not by oppressive inhumanism. Rosabeth Kanter (1972:1) defines utopia as "the imaginary society . . . where all physical, social, and spiritual forces work together, in harmony, to permit the attainment of everything people find necessary and desirable." There is contentment, happiness, and perfect adjustment—the good life with the maximum of pleasure, play, and abundance. The inference is that the satisfaction of human wants is attainable only through the eradication of radical evil.

There is a sense in which all social systems are utopian. Social systems draw their ideals not from the realm of what is, but from the realm of what might be, and they use these ideals to inspire collective activity, which aims to change reality to conform with their goals. By definition utopia is an imaginary land (literally, "no place") and according to David Plath (1971:8) a society not found in the *National Geographic Atlas.* But there are those who dream of finding it, determined to produce a society that will be utterly perfect. Robert Owen was such a dreamer and is now remembered more for his utopian socialism than for his actual accomplishments. Anthropologist A. L. Kroeber (1952:130) has observed this dichotomy between the dream and the reality by saying that "any fool could devise a more consistent social system than exists, but even a despot rarely can institute one."

COMMUNITARIAN SOCIETY

The communitarian tradition is the record of the individuals and groups who have attempted to live communally, sharing material goods and a common life style. This tradition reaches back into history before the birth of Christ to the time of the Essenes, who practiced a rigid communism of property in Palestine

(Howlett 1957). Later, in Christian times, monastic leaders such as St. Benedict and St. Francis held that the possession of private property was in contradiction with Christian teaching.

Nonconformist groups emerging before and after the Protestant Reformation often shared beliefs, property, and lives. These sects included the Cathars in France, the Lollards in England, the Labadists in Holland, the Waldenses in Italy, and the Anabaptists in various parts of Europe. In their return to the primitive Christian teachings that emphasized the Kingdom of God and the transformation of conditions in this world, they adopted communal sharing. Two of the better known groups are the Old Order Amish and the Hutterites, the survivors of sixteenth century Anabaptists who have retained remarkable self-contained communal values (for Case Studies see bibliography). They were among the most radical and for several centuries the most persecuted of the sects.

Communitarianism grew rapidly in the rich soil of American optimism and socialism in the nineteenth century. Some of the more impressive communities were those of the Shakers, Owenites, Rappites, Fourierists, and the settlements of Oneida and Amana. Based on the faith that man can remake his institutions by reasoned choice, these communitarians shared the idea of employing the small community as a creative social force to produce reform in society. They believed that men are essentially free to choose their own destinies, and, while deliberately experimental, their ventures often failed. Communities were thus living tests of communal hypotheses, defined in more than economic terms.

The American communitarians appear to fall into two groups: those "which are plainly *religious* in foundation and type of leadership," and those "which are apparently 'secular' in style and atmosphere" (Littell 1965:xviii). Frequently the religious communitarians went back to the *Book of Acts*, which provided them with a model in the communism of the apostolic church. They perceived themselves as reinstituting the ideal Christian community.

The Icarians, Owenites, and Llano illustrate the secular components of the communitarian tradition. Numerous authors call attention to the fact that a religious ideology is contributory to, but not a sufficient condition for, longevity. Holloway (1966:227) argues that "there must be some fundamental belief to which all members subscribe—a belief capable of sustaining them in all crises and uniting them in spite of minor dissensions . . . [it] must be ritualized until it provides a sanction for all conduct." Charismatic leaders were usually effective in generating enthusiastic cooperation. Some well-organized groups continued after the death of their leader, thus contradicting the common notion that communal attempts fold after the death of their founders.

In virtually all communitarian movements there is either an element of counterculture or outright rejection of the dominant culture. A "counterculture" (Roszak 1969; Horowitz *et al.,* 1972) comes into being "when people come to believe with utter finality that everything they have been taught to be true is in fact false" (Westhues 1972:40). Adherents may practice radical nonconformist ways as a reaction against the dominant society. Some may be extremely active politically, though most appear to be passive, condemning or mocking the dominant political order. Counterculture does not necessarily imply the founding of communes, however.

"Intentional commune," a term emerging from the modern Quaker tradition and designating first generational groups, differs little from the meaning of communitarian. Membership requirements tend to be informal and unwritten with varying degrees of rigidity. The intentional commune demands participation in a "total" way of life. This comprehensive sharing involves material goods, lodging facilities, income, family responsibilities, ideology, and social organization. Strong strains of cultural primitivism are present—the goal is a return to perfect harmony with nature, not its manipulation or exploitation. The orientation is toward Eden (paradise) rather than Utopia. Thus one finds among many a preoccupation with organic gardening and agrarian self-sufficiency in rustic settings. Modern technology is viewed as oppressive dehumanization.

An open atmosphere of acceptance pervades the intentional commune during the early stages. There is often a search for a personal self-awareness, acceptance, and expression. Affective expression of emotions and open honesty is valued. "Be what you are." Sexual codes and practices are less rigid than in straight society.

Many communes are "in process," having limited permanency. Their life span tends to be transient and short. There is much tripping and exchange among groups. The ideology is often little more than crude consensus, not formalized or well articulated. Modern intentional communes would probably all agree that the scale of society as currently organized is too large.

THE APPROACH OF ANTHROPOLOGY

What insights does anthropology bring to our understanding of communitarian societies? Encompassing "man and his achievements" anthropology can be both exciting and intellectually rewarding. People who understand human societies and their complexities have an edge on others who do not. Knowledge about human groups, whether in the jungle or in the city, past or present, is not only satisfying and perhaps entertaining, but invaluable as a way of adapting to the modern world. Having profound implications for all peoples, it offers perspective, breadth, and variation in viewing ourselves as one people among many peoples. We gain startling new knowledge about our own culture as we view the total lifeway of other human groups.

The anthropologist is concerned with an understanding of the total culture of a human group. For example, he is not concerned only with the exotic or with specific customs, but with the complex whole as it constitutes a way of life. To achieve this holistic understanding, the anthropologist must go to the natural settings to observe the life of the people. He must engage in conversations with them, listen to them talk, work and play with them, participate in their activities, and describe their cultural knowledge. The result is an *ethnography* (the description of a culture), not to be confused with *ethnology* (the classification, comparison, and explanation of several cultures).

Ethnographic detail is extremely important in cultural anthropology, for without it the anthropologist cannot classify, compare, and explain similarities and differences across all societies. The scope of the observations involves social patterns (social anthropology), including the interactions of people, their locations, and situations, as well as culture patterns (cultural anthropology), including all that members of a group need to know in order to participate fully in their society. The goal of the anthropologist is not simply to describe a people and their behavior from the viewpoint of trained observer, but to discover how the people view themselves. He must ask the question "What do these people see themselves doing?"

The approach to communitarians in this book is ethnographic, and its aim is to understand the social and cultural context of each community. We have chosen three communal groups representing different time periods and ideological perspectives. One group existed for scarcely three years, another for roughly one generation, and the third group has a history of over four centuries. Since they are so varied and since human nature in groups is infinitely complex and impossible to describe in complete detail, we shall focus the description around five core concepts: (1) origin (preconditions which brought the group into being), (2) ideology or professed beliefs (as distinguished from the dominant culture), (3) subsistence activity (basic resources used to satisfy hunger and other bodily needs), (4) social patterns (family and socialization), and (5) polity (internal forms of authority).

The three groups will be discussed in the order of their longevity, the briefest first. The group in existence the longest has had more experience with long-range problem solving and with building an environment that can cope with many of the problems of identity and survival. In contrast, the youngest group is the most unstable.

Communitarian societies, like all human cultures, attempt to provide a secure, continuous, and rewarding experience for their members. To be successful (we are not thinking only of longevity, but also of community self-realization) a communitarian group must take into account its relations with the outside world and structure its own operation so as to protect itself against intrusion or assimilation. Each of the three groups perceives and reacts to external conflict in different ways. In the concluding chapter we will discuss the major adaptations of each group and some of their similarities and differences.

2

The Family:
An Experiment in Group Marriage

"The Family," as they call themselves, is a contemporary commune founded in the late 1960s in the western part of the United States. Among the group were some highly skilled and educated young men and women who became involved in "raising consciousness." Their sincerity, high level of sophistication in dealing with intimate-personal space (proxemics), group marriage, and efforts to develop the potential of human awareness are a few of the "social engineering" attempts that merit our attention. Though the group has since fragmented after an unsuccessful financial venture, its achievements in altering social patterns are relevant for understanding modern communes. Of the three communitarian groups, the Family is probably the most difficult for the anthropologist to observe. The problem is not only one of fluidity (constant dynamic change) but the fact that social scientists and the scientific approach are suspect to many of the people who join the communes.[1] One communal spokesman put it this way: "We understand things through involvement—by doing. We are trying to break down the observer–observed dichotomy, and anyone who imposes that structure on us is going to miss what we're doing altogether." Speaking was a Ph.D. candidate in psychology, who dropped out from his graduate studies when he joined the group. He was pointing out one of the difficulties in an "objective study" of the Family.

The source of our descriptive data is a former participating member of the Family, Eric Michaels, who, with the aid of his anthropology instructors, reconstructed the essential features of the commune. To plan and execute a research design from the start of the commune would have been impossible because a scientifically trained observer would not have been tolerated in the group.

ORIGIN: CATACLYSMIC EXPECTATIONS

The history of the Family traces back to Berkeley, California, in 1966, during the period known as the "Summer of Love." Lord Byron was living at the time with a handful of young men and women in a small apartment. He sensed that

[1] Illustrations of the Family commune are intentionally omitted in this Basic Unit. The authors have respected the Family's desire to remain relatively anonymous and their feelings of distrust for academia.

there was going to be trouble in the Bay Area—the riots of Berkeley, possible earthquakes, the chaotic influx of hippies into Haight-Ashbury. Equipped with a few hundred dollars and the combined positive energy of the dozen or so members at the time, he parlayed the sum into $14,000 at the gambling tables in Reno. With the money, the group outfitted themselves with a large school bus and crossed the desert to Mesa, Arizona, a middle-class suburb of Phoenix, where they rented a home and began "The Family."

Lord Byron related to the members in a personal, conversational way—perhaps as a benevolent father figure—but more accurately as a peer with special decision-making roles. In Mesa the Family's activities were confined to the usual sort of hippie coffee-house and merchandising experiments.

During the first year at Mesa, the Family began to establish a truly alternative life style and to deal with the problems of resocializing its own members into new structures. In terms of the group marriage, this was the period when the problems of jealousy and hostility were confronted. The size of the group was approximately 35 to 40 members, including the initial core of 25 people from Berkeley, augmented by about a dozen frequently changing peripheral members, who would stay from a few weeks to a few months and then leave. The distribution of men to women remained nearly equal throughout the history of the Family, except for a few brief periods when there was an acute shortage of women. The size of the Family fluctuated throughout its history, but 75 people were about the maximum for efficiency.

Following the move to Mesa there was continual splintering of the group. The process involved a small number of peripheral members, occasionally with the support of a single core member, who would decide that the goals of the group could be best implemented outside of the jurisdiction of Lord Byron (although this was not the only reason and rarely the one given). These "houses," as they were called, were usually short-lived, anywhere from a month to a year, at which point they would disband, with several members returning to the Family, the rest usually resorting to one of the other options that the hip world offered at the time.

The splintering and turnover of the peripheral members were not seen until much later as threatening to the group. The process was considered a necessary step, both in personal development (splinterers had certain unfulfilled desires to work out before their commitment could be total) and in terms of the need for new members in order to keep the self-image of the group from stagnation.

One Christmas day a "Family gathering" was held, in which past and present members and several splinter houses gathered in Taos, New Mexico, to celebrate the holiday season. Most of the Mesa core group made the trip, and the most influential members, next to Lord Byron, were impressed by the combination of scenery, spirituality, and communal development that centered in this small mountain village of 4000 people. Against what Lord Byron later referred to as his "better judgment," the group decided to relocate in Taos, and by Spring the Family was re-established.

During the nearly two years in Taos, the group developed a more structured identity that came to be recognizably distinct from the other communes in the area. Additionally, the existence of Taos as a well-publicized center for communal activity influenced the behavior of the group. Relations with neighboring communes, with a largely hostile local population, and with large numbers of young urban exiles presented a new set of problems that were both indigenous to the area and, at the same time, microcosmically indicative of the relation of communes to the dominant society at that time.

One hundred members were considered more than the maximum for functioning as a single household, and the membership was increasing steadily. In February of 1970 there were 49 members, including 8 children. By late Spring the number had increased to nearly 100, including 14 children, 8 cats, 5 goats, and 9 dogs, and an arsenal of about 10 rifles, shotguns, and pistols. At the time, however, the entire household was living in a two-bedroom, adobe house designed for about 3 people.

There was still the crisis caused by turnover, and it seemed to demand new solutions. Ugly scenes in neighboring communes had resulted from FBI infiltration in the area and from the influx of a less committed kind of summer hippie. In addition, the group felt that the Family's success required the total energy of its committed members. A more selective screening process was agreed upon: The previous acceptance of all prospective members and the past inhibitions regarding the expulsion of a member were now amended.

The group next faced a series of enormous threats to its survival. A good deal of money had been invested on a documentary film the Family had made during the Winter and Spring. Half the members had spent the Summer touring the country in an attempt to distribute the film and realize a financial gain from it. By midsummer, however, the overhead expense for the film was greater than the profits, and there was no money to support the various Family enterprises. Added to the financial problems was the fact that the people who went on the road returned frequently with their beliefs badly shaken, and they required considerable support. Furthermore, "reliable sources" had indicated that in the wake of the Charles Manson publicity a state crackdown on communes was about to begin. At this point, Lord Byron made another trip to Reno in an attempt to repeat his previous performance but met with less success. The Family packed up and got ready to move, divided into a traveling unit of about twenty people (most of the original core and women with children) and the other members, who were sent off individually or in small groups. While the core group sought a new location, the others were to attempt to locate money and were given a number of other tasks. They would notify the members when a home had been found; by Thanksgiving, everyone who still claimed membership was to come to the new location. What followed was a series of short migrations through Northern California, Colorado, Utah, following "leads" that eventually ended up in a midwest city. When the participant-observer ended contact with the Family it was still thriving, and there were few major changes in either the core personnel, size, or values of the group. We will now attempt to reconstruct the ideology, polity, subsistence patterns, and social patterns of the Family.

IDEOLOGY: RAISING CONSCIOUSNESS

Youth communes are commonly identified and described by the ideological beliefs they manifest. Even within the youth culture, a given group will be identified as a macrobiotic commune, a radical-political commune, a back-to-the-land commune, and so on. Although such gross descriptions are not always accurate enough for ethnographic purposes, they provide a logical point of entry into the rather complicated set of events and beliefs under discussion.

The Family was characterized primarily as a group marriage. However, a group marriage is not properly an ideology, but a methodology. Like all methods used by the Family, even this one was considered nothing more than an expedient toward altering consciousness and socialization.

The avowed ideological goal of the group was to be a society that transcended the usual limitations of individuals. Members believed it possible that an individual's self-awareness could maximize his human potential and that, through the application of certain techniques and disciplines basic to many religions and philosophies, they could develop such an awareness. As an aid the group maintained a rather extensive library, which included works of the world's major religions, philosophies, and psychologies. The unique, underlying bias of the Family, however, was that the proper way to create self-aware individuals was through a specialized group or community epitomized by group marriage. This social structure had its philosophical root in the sense of marriage as communion with another person or, in this case, persons.

Since the Family was determined to avoid dogma, and since methodologies were considered temporary, members agreed that the form of group marriage might one day be abandoned when they "got beyond that point." Although an observer might doubt that this central structure could be replaced successfully, the belief in the *experimental* use of methodologies was also central to the group identity. It served to distinguish the group from neighboring communes, who were said to be trapped in one dogma or another.

The approach to everything from diet to faith healing was a flexible and casual form of empirical method. In terms of the organizational structure the "try it—if it works, keep it—for as long as it works" method was frequently used as a way of intensifying a structure that developed informally. In addition, there was a certain value in experiencing systems with which individual members were either unfamiliar or, especially, uncomfortable. Through this inverse approach members, who were frequently refugees from authoritarian hierarchies, were expected to function in an authoritarian experiment.

As might be expected, antagonism sometimes developed. In a subculture where hostility was avoided by a display of two fingers (the peace sign), the Family placed a high value on confronting hostilities. Fist fights were not uncommon and were actually considered beneficial. It was rare for a fight to be broken up, or even disturb other people in the room, except for one or two outsiders who would enter the interaction in conciliatory roles as witnesses. It was believed that triadic interaction was less likely to become stagnant than a diad, and hostilities would often be dealt with by several members of the group who were not directly involved.

At times, specific methods were used for dealing with problems. A specific form of Gestalt therapy, developed largely by Fritz Perls at Esalen Institute, was adapted for use by the group.[2] To anyone familiar with Perls' work, the combination of group interaction and keeping experience in the "here and now" would obviously be very attractive to the Family. During the year that Gestalt therapy was most popular, a group of five to fifteen people would be called together to sit down and publicly perform their dreams, anxieties, and secrets. Later this method was replaced by others, notably group exercises and group meditation. Terms from these various disciplines remained in the daily jargon and were used as shortcuts in conversation. Over time, a specialized terminology and a specialized group of concerns came to distinguish the group from other communes. Such a Family line might contain one or more of the following beliefs:

1. Self-development is a process that must be entered into with determination and commitment. It is the hardest thing one can do, and the only work truly worthy of man.
2. The group functions as a series of mirrors to reflect one's own behavior and implement the above process.
3. Possessions delude the individual into identifying with an artificial and external sense of oneself. Objects should be regarded in terms of usefulness, not ownership, and "cut loose" when no longer used.
4. Ownership of people (seen as a hangup of capitalistic systems) destroys the human potential in both parties involved.
5. Awareness is a refined degree of perception and is likened to the workings of a well-oiled machine. It is the ability to track a wide range or processes simultaneously, determine which needs attention, zoom in on it, and shift gears to perform the task at hand.

Although unique in many ways, the Family did share certain beliefs and life styles with other communes. These shared beliefs were related to an apocalyptic vision that was prevalent during the late sixties among many young Americans. The common ground for hippies during this time was drug use, cosmetological preferences, and a specialized jargon. Within this larger group, there was a sizable body of people who believed that either the world was coming to an end or that it was approaching some almost unimaginable change of a cataclysmic nature. Opinions varied on whether the change would be triggered by human causes such as ecological poisoning or war, natural disasters such as earthquakes or landslides, or

---

[2] Important works in the library of the commune included: Fritz Perls, *Gestalt Therapy Verbatim*; G. I. Gurdieff, *Meetings with Remarkable Men* and *All and Everything*; and R. Heinlien, *Stranger in a Strange Land*. A number of other books by such diverse authors as Abraham Maslow, Robert Rimmer, Theodore Sturgeon, and Carl Jung passed in and out of popularity. Books of the major literate religions of the world were important, especially the *Aquarian Gospel* on Tarot, Astrology, and other systems of divination. *Lao Tsu Ching* was a frequently quoted source. Subscriptions included the *Wall Street Journal, Life, Popular Mechanics, Scientific American*, and the *Whole Earth Catalog*. A separate file was kept on contemporary and underground books, especially those that dealt with the communal movement.

some supernatural event such as the Second Coming. In most cases, these forecasts were combined to create a rather frightening picture of the near future. However, the general belief was that beyond the cataclysm lay an infinitely better world—either an Aquarian age or a re-emergence of Atlantis. These beliefs gave experimental societies a great sense of urgency. Faced with a larger social order that many of these people found unsatisfying or even immoral, it seemed necessary to create small societies of alternative structures and values to experiment with many possibilities.

Within the network of "alternative societies," certain identifying features came to be common to most groups, including the Family. One of the most widely recurring topics was food—from the preparation of soil to the planting, growing, preparing of meals, and the etiquette of the hippie or communal table. Food was always regarded in terms of its organic pedigree, that is, how "naturally" it had been dealt with at all stages. Although the Family disavowed the organic dogma, the inordinate amount of concern that it paid to food intake was still apparent in nutritional and economic terms. A second common concern was intergroup gossip. Visitors would often be quizzed at length about the fate of other communes and individuals both in the area and in other centers of youth culture development. Even when this topic became institutionalized by the Family at its information center, discussions at home would often be about other groups or other individuals. Relations with both the authorities and the local working class were often considered important.

Occult systems and divination were common not only to the Family but were shared with many youth groups. The amount of attention and the degree of expertise in the Family, however, was probably greater than in most groups. A visitor would often be asked his astrological sign before being asked his name, and the I Ching was consulted before any major decision was made. Visionary dreams, extrasensory perception, and manifestations of "supernatural" knowledge were highly prized. Members entertained a wide range of legends and theories that were commonly related to a single theory of history dating back to the legendary lost continent of Atlantis. This theory was offered as an alternative to traditional western-political history and as both an origin and unifying element for the wide range of apparently contradictory systems held by various members. Reincarnations were discussed at length, and there were those who theorized that all the members of the present group had at one time known each other on the Atlantean continent. The single difference between the Family's use of these systems and other groups' was that the actual truth of the legends or systems was unimportant. Astrology, for instance, was not a deterministic system but a gridwork through which to structure perceptions. Alternative interpretations of any system were possible, and often discussion would revolve around attempts to synthesize modern philosophy and science with other less "respectable" systems.

The Family spoke of itself as a school, a sort of training ground for the Aquarian age. There was a somewhat mystical notion of the group organism as a magic circle—a pool of energies that could work miracles—complete as long as no member of the circle doubted (drained energy from) the whole. This placed a certain strain on members who would often feel disproportionately responsible for failure. And though the group spoke of itself as not unique but merely one node, or manifestation of, a whole global change in consciousness and behavior, they were aware of their own in-group defensiveness. When this was fed back to them (through their various film or tape work of meetings with other local communes) the idea of re-establishing the us–them boundaries of the hippie society made everyone very uncomfortable. But as the care of individual egos was the concern of the group more than Lord Byron, the care of the group ego was left in his hands, since no one else felt qualified to deal with it.

The people held in highest esteem outside of the Family were not mystics, with which the New Mexico region abounds and which other hippie groups find so attractive. Most mystics, when measured against the Family value scale, were considered to be "out of touch with their bodies," "talking double-talk," or simply "small time" (i.e., ineffectual as world saviors). The few outsiders who passed Family scrutiny and were taken into confidence included a magazine editor, a movie actor, an avant-garde electronics engineer, a visual anthropologist, a psychic researcher, and a medical intern. All were successful in their fields, and all recognized some sort of kinship with the group. The Family had no time for failures, nor for the hippie society that had disavowed challenge because of what was assessed as a fear of failure.

The Family considered itself a bridge to a new evolutionary age that would feature groups of three or more people functioning as a single organism (*homo gestalt*) through a policy of nonpossession. As has been seen, a blending of mystical terms and pragmatic idealism made the group remarkably different from the back-to-the-land communes in the area, and the emphasis on group marriage and bodily awareness made them distinct from most other contemporary religious or apocalyptic communes. As an esoteric school, they devoted themselves to process and experience in a vigorous way, disavowing dogma. Their belief system was thus supported by an unusual but uneven degree of sophistication about their place in terms of both historical antecedents and contemporary society.

SUBSISTENCE: ECONOMIC AND PRODUCTIVE ACTIVITIES

Economics, although of great concern to the Family, was the area in which they reaped the least satisfactory results. Lord Byron, as the head of the economic household, made all decisions regarding major expenditures. Money was viewed in terms of his theory, "The Forward Flow of Money," as "packaged energy," a McLuhanesque term. When stagnant—that is, stored in banks or invested in useless possessions, money was wasted. Instead, the Family used cash on hand to buy tools, especially those that would accrue more money.

Money flowed through the Taos area in a variety of rather complicated ways. Except for the tourist industry there was little incoming cash in the area (one of the poorest in the U.S.). Jobs that were unrelated to the Family philosophy, that required the members to work as individuals or to relate mainly to co-workers outside the group were shunned. Instead, Lord Byron tapped, the one real source of capital in the area—the young, insecure, hippie millionaires. One of the local hippie heirs was persuaded to invest a sizable percentage of his personal fortune in a complex of service projects that would be run by the Family. A corporate structure was set up to manage a free clinic, a general store, and an information center for the Taos area. The group would plan and staff these operations, all housed in a single modern structure, with an eye to eventually turning the work over to the community as a whole. As a result, members now had a series of salaried jobs consistent with their values, and their own needs for food and health care could be met at minimum cost. The general store would recoup the losses of the other two operations, and lecture fees would provide additional income.

The scheme appeared to be a relatively clever one. However, due to the near epidemic proportion of illnesses among the new arrivals in the area, the medicine and staff were insufficient. When it was realized that the original sum designated for these services would be gone within a year, Lord Byron proposed "the Corporation," in which the Family had the voting majority. A grand plan was developed —the group would sell information in the form of a documentary movie and a magazine. The plan was approved and developed into a full-length documentary on the communes of the Taos region. The best available equipment was rented from Hollywood; in the process, plans for the magazine, to be called *Euspychia*, and for other projects were removed from consideration. Over the next six months the movie was filmed, edited, and processed at a tremendous cost due to ineffectual administration and the unfamiliarity of the members with the technology involved in film making.

To understand how a group could go through what eventually turned out to be nearly a quarter of a million dollars (a somewhat exaggerated but convenient figure) in a six-month period, and produce what was later considered a remarkably bad film, it is necessary to appreciate the certainty and unshakable optimism of the Family. They saw technology as a minor impediment to the final result, and believed that a positive and conscientious approach to the tools would guarantee a worthy project. But it turned out that the group had overestimated its technical sophistication and, more centrally, consistently misunderstood both the subculture of the area and the way it could be communicated via the film to another culture (the movie-going public).

The optimism of the group made it impossible to abandon the film, and further funds were secured for an elaborate promotional tour, the results of which sapped the last financial sources of the group, ran up a huge pile of debts, strained relations with the community, and precipitated a crisis among the membership. The tour also led to the group's migration to a midwestern city, an uneasy relationship with collection agencies and the law, and the dispersal of nearly half of the members.

In terms of experience the venture was worthwhile. Certain parties had been persuaded to underwrite the film, and since most of the creditors were corporations with sizable assets, no single person, it was reasoned, had actually been hurt on the human-personal level. It is worth noting that an offer to recut the film and provide a narration, made by a qualified and famous friend of the group, was turned down. Ideologically, the offer violated the work ethic of the group, which stated that all products of the Family must be joint efforts by members of the commune only.

Personal possessions were minimal and transient. Although each member might have a collection of personal effects (a "stash"), including clothing, toilet articles, and a few mementoes or bits of jewelry, a month later he might have none of those articles. When a person joined the Family, it was explained to him that all his money and goods would have to be surrendered, and this transference was usually effected within a week or two. People often hoarded some spare change, but amounts over a dollar were usually given up; if it was discovered that a person had a bank account or liquid assets, pressure was placed on him to relinquish them. Certain tools, however, might be placed under a given person's jurisdiction, and he had the right to withhold use of them. If a person was sloppy with his tools or his few possessions, he would be rebuked.

It is difficult to separate what the Family viewed as its economic patterns from its ideology and social structure. Because it aimed at integrating all aspects of life in a single flow of process, a description of one time period cannot represent the consistent pattern of institutionalization that is evident only from a longer study. In summation, however, the economic system was compatible with the value pattern. The processes of production were paramount to the final product on its value scale. The structure and style of a corporation were adopted, allowing it to parlay large sums of money without actually having any. Other factors made the economic system difficult for outsiders to comprehend. Niches in the bureaucratic structure were retained, as were job roles, but personnel were free to circulate through these structures; workers were expected to consider themselves expendable and able to perform most roles. Also unique was the fact that a person's development was a better qualification for a position than his ability or even interest in the job.

SOCIAL PATTERNS: SOCIALIZATION AND LIVING PATTERNS

The Family's designation of itself as a group marriage was taken literally by the members. The practice of group marriage distinguished the Family from most other contemporary communal groups of its size and duration. In practice it is almost as if the basic composition of the American nuclear family were multiplied by thirty; many of the same values remained, but the size and variety of relationships added an entirely different dimension. Members referred to each other as husbands and wives, and children were regarded as having many fathers and mothers.

In actuality, not everybody slept with everybody else (although a variety of opinions existed as to the desirability of such an arrangement). The beds were allocated to the women, who had the choice to accept or reject a sleeping partner, whether for sex or companionship, for the evening. Within this basic set of rules, promiscuity was avoided. Women frequently maintained a small circle of sleeping partners, which might vary from time to time. Couples evolved but not in the usual sense. While a member's partner might sleep with and even make love to a number of other people during a week, the member knew that they would spend several nights together and frequently share activities during the day.

A man's woman, if he had one, could be distinguished as the person who kept his personal effects near her bed and would check to make sure his laundry got downstairs if he weren't home that day. Women and men who exercised no discrimination in sleeping partners, and couples who would allow no other partners were remarked about. The latter case usually was brought under group scrutiny if the couple persisted with an exclusive arrangement for a long period of time; the two would be advised on the basis of their own development as to whether they ought to continue the arrangement. No one was ever told to have intercourse with someone else. However, sleeping arrangements might be manipulated either by group pressure or, rarely, by Lord Byron. There was a certain value placed on the mere act of sleeping beside another person. On occasion, even two males who were not getting along might be advised to sleep together, although the taboo on homosexuality was fairly rigid.

Sleeping took place in large dormitory rooms, and privacy was unknown. Yet group sex was almost never tried or even suggested. On the other hand, the sense of humor of the group included a third party's running commentary in the dark on a couple's performance. The effect of this lack of privacy, which might strike terror into a properly socialized American's heart, had an unusually therapeutic effect on the group. A person's sex life was a public matter and somehow was handled with taste, sensitivity, and concern. Some who had opted for a deviant sex role in the straight culture performed happily within these norms.

The question of parenthood of a given child was usually considered irrelevant. Mothers remained closest to their biological children during the first year, when lactation took place. After that, too close an involvement with a child, to the exclusion of other children in the group, might bring a mother under group censure. Despite the admission that there were no available models for child rearing along Family lines, the children seemed healthy.

The oldest child in the group was six years old. She was attending a local private school because there were not enough children her age to play with and because peer group relations were considered important to a child's development. (The public schools in the area preached outright hate toward the local communes, and it was considered suicidal to send a child there.) The rest of the children were directed by a member who was a certified teacher and by a rotating group of assistants, who provided play space and toys.

Members did not seek to perpetuate the group by child rearing. At a certain point in the development of the group's ideology, it was determined that the attempt to make the world better for the sake of the children was a ploy used by straight people to deal with their own failure, and to "lay a trip on the kids." In fact it was joked that these children would probably rebel against their parents by going to college. The Family intended to fulfill their own dreams. This being the case, the children were considered free to develop their own.

There was a conflict between those members of the group who advocated traditional child-rearing methods and those who advocated a progressive approach. The limitations on space, as well as the disciplined nature of the group, made progressive methods inappropriate. Most of the central members were content with a more traditional form of child rearing that included a certain degree of corporal punishment. The indeterminate nature of authority in the group itself frequently created problems when two people tried to discipline the same child by different methods. Children were a new experience with the Family, and methods were expected to stabilize in time.

The socialization rituals were reserved for new members. On entering the commune the person would be confronted by a large number of people, usually at work or in conversation. The members were remarkable in the wide variety of types and dress, while avoiding the extremes of costuming popular in the area. Noticeably, the group looked animated, happy, healthy, and their hair was kept conservatively short. Individually, the members were taken for college-age ski tourists or vacationing newlyweds when they walked around town. This was in marked contrast both to the way the rest of the communes looked and the way most of them had appeared earlier. Usually a few people would separate themselves from the group and, after identifying themselves, engage the person in conversation.

Walking into the Family house was often a disturbing experience for a stranger. Imagine a small dwelling designed to accomodate an average nuclear family now transformed into the living quarters for 60 or 70 men, women, and children. To outsiders the arrangement was unbearably crowded. Bunkbeds lined the walls of every room except the kitchen. In the corner stood stacks of mattresses that would be used at night to cover any empty floor space. The effect was of one huge party. If we consider Edward Hall's (1959:146–164) proxemics model (the use of space in communication), it becomes apparent that the Family lived almost constantly in personal and intimate space, as opposed to the larger American culture, which lives in social and impersonal space. Territoriality was minimal, especially for the men, who could claim no rights to any given space. Yet this arrangement suited the Family members quite well. They were aware of the results of this crowding and believed that the effects were conducive to and in keeping with their ideology, for the small house made secrecy, individualism, and capitalism impossible within the' group. Until a crisis was reached in which the membership was increased to 100, suggestions to move into a larger space were never welcomed. This is significant because anthropologists have noticed that cultures use space differently and that privacy is not considered beneficial or even necessary in all cultures. In this one remarkable way, the Family may have done more to create a radical departure from its parent culture than any of the more overt disciplines it practiced.

If it was determined that a person was interested in joining the group, he might be taken directly to Lord Byron or to someone else who would give him an explanation of what was going on in the Family. Visitors and prospective members alike had to be screened by Byron for security reasons, since the Family was quick to make its system known and "psyche out" a person at the same time. Often the new visitor would be asked for cigarettes and money, a gesture whereby the group was both acknowledging its socialist economy and aping the hippie beggars. Later the practice was stopped when it was decided that it wasn't funny any more. Usually those aspects of the Family that were least palatable to a "trippie" (i.e., a hippie with no sense of commitment) were presented first. These included the no-drug rule, the idea of hard work, and the necessary initiation ritual of the haircut. If a person passed these tests, the interviewer would then ease him off the spot a bit, discussing the Family and selecting liberally from the maxims connected with the ideology.

The required haircut was perhaps the most effective selection device the group used. Short hair had been decided upon after the first year in Taos to ease tension with the locals: A member who was inconspicuous was less likely to incur the hostility of a "hippie-hater" than would a longhair. It was also an attempt to make a break with the hippie ethic and life style from which most of the members recently had come. In asking a newcomer to cut his hair you were asking him to make a break with his familiar identity symbol and accept the norms of the group. The request effectively screened out over half the applicants. Since the group frequently made extreme demands on the individual, it was an excellent introductory ritual. After this was accepted, the communal economic system was made clear—no personal holdings. The rest of an interview was dedicated to finding out about the person, his personality, background, and skills. This was done in a highly anecdotal style. At the end, the person would be introduced to a few people he might find it easy to get along with quickly, and directed to an activity in which to become immediately involved.

Members quickly take on personal roles with the individual and guide him through the first days of immersion. Someone will kindly explain the rituals and perform introductions, and another may make immediate demands on him. There is usually a session of scouting around for a new name. (Taking a new name and changing one's appearance on entering the Family quickly upsets a person's self-image.) Since the Family sees static self-images as counterproductive, this quick method of uprooting a person is highly effective.

Shortly after arrival (perhaps a day or two) the person would be called into an encounter session, where he would be expected to open himself to observation on a personal level to a sample of members. Frequently any hangups that have been observed by members at this time will be ferreted out—shyness, aversion to nudity, possessiveness (hoarding), and other behaviors that need to be altered to conform to the group. Sometimes these sessions become highly emotional or blocked as the person is put in an unusually awkward situation; in some cases they evolve into a more casual sort of discussion. These initial sessions are considered useful for both the individual and the group, since the group has a chance to see itself commented on by an interested person who has not yet become socialized into the structure. Eventually this form of therapy was largely abandoned, but for some time it was a central tool for both socializing and therapy.

After the first few days, the new member begins to slip into the routine of the group. He finds a job and establishes a small circle of friends. He is not allowed to make love to the women until a week or so has passed and until he has been checked for V.D. (a process that has both medical and social advantages). The only really disturbing problem that may be common to every new member, besides the rule (hardly rigid) that everybody must take orders from everybody else, is that his circle of friends may slip away from him or that perfect strangers may approach him and demand, "Why don't you care about me?" or something to that effect. There is a rhythm, set of gestures, and vocabulary shared by the group, which has to be learned over time; until this happens, the person remains an outsider. Adjustment to these quickly changing patterns of closeness, "in" behavior, and the previously mentioned lack of private space cause something of a culture shock in this society. All space in the Family is multifunctional, and the proxemics of this society are astonishing in that there are probably more people within one's intimate space than in any other conceivable group.

There is one more rite enacted on the personal level—the acquisition of a title. At one point in the Family's history, it was decided that people were taking each other for granted. To increase respect among members, all people took the title of Lord or Lady. Later the categories of Sir and Mistress were added to designate members who had not yet achieved full commitment to the group. Titling was usually done by Lord Byron at dinnertime, but in certain cases a person would acquire the title through a particular set of deeds and the ritual would be anti-climactic. Occasionally a member would be demoted—usually in an attempt to humble someone who had become too authoritarian. Also, members who left and later returned to the group were not immediately restored to their title.

POLITY: INTERNAL AUTHORITY AND LEADERSHIP

In retrospect it is difficult to understand how decisions were made in the Family. The group's own statement that decisions were arrived at by "intuitive consensus" is not to be taken absolutely when we understand the function of Lord Byron as group leader. Yet to explain the polity of the Family as a bureaucratic hierarchy with Byron at the head is also inaccurate. Between group consensus and autocracy there was a continuum for making decisions, depending upon the way the group saw itself at any particular time.

Ideally the Family functioned as a heterarchy, defined as a group whose structure is flexible so as to permit the person with the most expertise in a given task to function as a leader for that task and then to revert back to the baseline of equality. In reality, however, Lord Byron exercised veto power over any decision, though he rarely exercised his power except in matters relating to the survival of the group as a whole. In this sense he was economic head of the Family. Jobs, projects, and expenditures would have to be cleared through him, and would often originate with him. He found it necessary to maintain a private space in the house, and when this was not possible he would reside nearby in order to have this privilege. Positions of authority were frequently given to new members who exhibited unusual skill. However, membership at the policy-making level was not granted to anyone until he had spent a long time with the group and had exhibited his commitment to the satisfaction of Lord Byron. Decisions were generally made after dinner, the main ritual of the day, when the group would air their impressions as well as sing, dance, and have personal interest workshops. In this way the integration of work and play with the events of the day was achieved.

All members of the Family were expected to be able to change jobs at a moment's notice, but male and female roles remained much the same as the middle-class society from which most of the members came. When women who had been exposed to the women's liberation movement entered the group, they frequently found adjustment difficult for it was argued that the situation of a woman was radically different from her counterpart in "straight" society. This being the case, women's lib was inappropriate. Men were responsible exclusively in matters of group security, although they did the dishes and helped care for the children. Women generally did the cooking and laundry. In fact, the role of the man as provider and protector was fairly rigid, and few women ever entered into the policy-making sessions of the group. There were separate men's and women's meetings weekly at least, and the stratification of certain tasks along sexual lines was rarely broken.

The effect of this social structure was to create a tightly knit group of people who were more personally involved with a larger number of people than is common in urban society in America. Since it was nearly impossible to maintain intimate relations with fifty people simultaneously, a sort of rotating closeness evolved in which members had a primary circle of intimates that changed slowly over time. Members were constantly keeping a check on all other members, and if a relationship seemed to be deteriorating with any other person, both were required to "get it on." It was said, "We are as far apart from each other as the two most hostile members are." If the rift continued, other members would attempt to effect a confrontation. At first this was informal, but if the rift continued, more and more structured methods would be used. Encounter groups, a variety of games, sleeping together, and working on the same project were all methods used to this end. The application of such sessions was highly idiosyncratic, but the basic form is recognizable as a highly concentrated way of bringing a person face-to-face with himself.

An example of a group confrontation occurred between Lord George and the film crew, who had a difficult time working with each other. Three members who went to the West Coast with him to do the final film editing came back quite shaken by the quality of the relationships that evolved among them during that period. During one session in the commune's film room while promotional strategy was being worked out, the hostilities flared up again. Everyone then sat down in the middle of the room and went into therapeutic gear—that is, prepared to confront the problem. First, the film was placed in the center of the room (a work print, the only copy at this point). One member laid down the rules for the session, " 'If anybody feels, at any point, that this film is going to tear us apart—there's the film, there's a match. Burn it.' Then we went around the room, describing how we felt about the film, how we felt about each other." At one point in this session, one woman broke down and grabbed the film. Lord George (who had in this session identified very heavily with the film) chased her through the hall. There was a lot of shouting and probably some hitting. Everyone held his breath, hoping that the $100,000 investment wouldn't have to go up in smoke. It didn't. Lord George and the woman returned arm-in-arm. The film making was marked by more than the usual number of such sessions, but the peace was only temporary. The final failure of the film was attributed to the fact that the crew was never able to resolve their hostilities, and that in this case, the sessions acted only as temporary remedies.

Only in rare cases, such as when a rift threatened to affect production or cause a member to consider leaving, did Lord Byron enter into the matter. On the whole, personal interaction was considered best handled on the casual level, and personal problems on the group level. The effect of having fifty people constantly minding your business seems like an extraordinary intrusion to most people, but was a comfortable situation in the context of this group. The effect, therefore, was minimal alienation and maximal integration with peers.

3

The Oneida Community:
Perfection and Scientific Propagation

The *second* communitarian society in our book, Oneida, was formed in the New England states during the nineteenth century. During its life span from 1848 until 1880 there were never more than 306 members. Perfection in human society was believed possible through personal communication with God, where members share all personal possessions and live as one family by practicing complex marriage. As in the Family, extensive use was made of mutual criticism, and the children were raised by the community. Financial success was achieved through industrial production, beginning with animal traps. Oneida thrived for a generation (32 years), and today exists as a joint-stock company.

The sources of our data are several historical accounts based upon the papers, records, and publications left by the members of the society. Diane Levy Miller assisted in the research and wrote the original draft of this chapter. The authors benefited from the helpful suggestions and criticisms of Maren Lockwood Carden (1969), who has written extensively on Oneida.

ORIGIN: THE IDEALISM OF A SEMINARY STUDENT

John Humphrey Noyes was the founder and spiritual leader of Oneida. Born in 1811 in Brattleboro, Vermont, "of respectable parents" (Nordhoff 1965:250), he graduated from Dartmouth in 1830 and then took up the study of law. In 1831 he entered the Andover Theological Seminary, and he was licensed to preach in 1833. In the following year Noyes strayed from traditional Christian dogma toward a doctrine of Perfectionism. Perfectionism meant for Noyes that the Second Coming of Christ had already occurred at the time of the fall of Jerusalem in 70 A.D., and "since that date all had been in readiness for the eventual perfection of this earthly life" (Lockwood 1965:185). He did not believe in the traditional view of sin or in the idea of eternal damnation. Anyone could be perfect if he accepted Christ into his soul, a spiritual state in which one could progress through degrees of perfection. He believed that society was evolving toward perfection, so that the kingdom of heaven would eventually exist on earth.

Due to his deviation from traditional Christian doctrine, Noyes lost his church

The Mansion House in Kenwood, N.Y., built in 1861 and owned by Oneida Ltd. Silversmiths, is now retained for the exclusive use of guests. (Photo courtesy of Oneida, Ltd.)

standing in 1834. Near Putney, Vermont, he began to practice and teach Perfectionism to a small "family of followers." The group called themselves the Putney Association and began to publish a religious newsletter, *The Witness*, in 1843. Its purpose was to help educate several confederated associations in the virtue of practicing the family spirit of the gospel through communal living.

The Perfectionist group owned 50 acres, seven buildings, a store, and a printing office in Putney. It was here that Noyes published in 1847 a compilation of his writings in *The Berean*, which later became the bible of Oneida communitarianism. After a series of hostile actions from the neighbors in Putney, Noyes and the Putney Association were driven out. They regrouped at Oneida, New York, in 1848, with the followers of John Burt, who had been a disciple of Noyes.

By 1853, Oneida was comprised of 250 acres, 130 persons in residence including 40 children, with horticulture, commerce, and peddling as the main pursuits. Four satellite communities also existed: Brooklyn, New York; Wallingford, Connecticut; Newark, New Jersey; and Cambridge, Vermont. By 1855 all the population was concentrated at either Oneida or Wallingford, with small gatherings of noncommunal Perfectionists in other states.

The physical development of Oneida was slow. Originally there were two log houses, later supplemented by a large brick Mansion House built in 1861. All members, most of whom were New England farmers and mechanics, with some teachers, lawyers, clergy, physicians, and merchants, lived in the Mansion House, where there were excellent recreation facilities, central heating, dining areas, and a children's wing. Other buildings included a school, barns, craft shops, and stables. By 1878 the community had grown to 306 people.

IDEOLOGY: SPIRITUAL PERFECTION LEADS TO COMMUNAL SHARING

The central beliefs in Oneida were self-perfection and "communalism." Self-perfection involved "the improvement of one's spiritual state, one's character, and one's intellect," and "communalism entailed sharing everything in the community" (Carden 1969:xiii). Salvation was not regarded as "a system of duty-doing under a code of dry laws," but as "a special phase of religious experience, having for its basis spiritual intercourse with God" (Nordhoff 1965:270). True perfection could only be achieved outside or away from the influence of the larger society. Communism was, therefore, necessary for the proper execution of Perfectionism.

The doctrine of Perfectionism was perpetuated by the distribution of the *Circular*, a daily newsletter of business, social events, and ideology. The *Circular* of January 17, 1854, lists the beliefs in the Perfectionists' "Theocratic Platform":

1. Sovereignty of Jesus Christ, dating from his Second Coming, A.D. 70, and sovereignty of the Primitive Church, raised from the dead at the Second Coming.
2. Unity of all Believers, in this world and in Hades, with the one Kingdom in the Heavens.
3. Resurrection of the spirit, overcoming Disease, renewing youth, and abolishing Death.
4. Community of property of all kinds, with inspiration for distribution.
5. Dwelling together in Association or Complex Families.
6. Home churches and Home schools.
7. Meetings every evening.
8. Lord's Supper at every meal.
9. Free Criticism the regulator of Society.
10. Horticulture the leading business for subsistence.
11. A daily press divorced from Mammon and devoted to God.

"Communalism" stood for the ideal of unity and immortality. Noyes wanted a system in which the happiness of the group would be more important to the individual than personal well-being. He believed in a spirit of love, a pattern close to that of the early Christian Church. By devoting oneself to the establishment of the Kingdom of God, the renunciation of private property, and by accepting Christ into the inner self, the individual could achieve control over the outer self. Then, through intercourse with God, selfishness would be destroyed and the body as well as the soul becomes immortal.

Picking currants at Oneida. Men and women shared in the work, whether in the fields or in the kitchen. (Photo courtesy of Oneida, Ltd.)

Noyes was not satisfied with merely handing down general principles, for he had very specific doctrines about virtually every aspect of life. Through speeches, home-talks, printed newsletters, and traditions, the members of the Oneida Community developed a set of principles that were specific as well as generally dogmatic. The practical application of the ideology is illustrated in the several phases of social organization.

SUBSISTENCE: HORTICULTURE AND SMALL INDUSTRY

The community drew its initial adherents from New England farmers and workers. New members brought all their personal capital with them and signed it over to the community, which at first existed almost solely from farming and horticulture. The first few years were marked by economic hardship, for farming was crude, and the other businesses of logging and swamp clearing were not very rewarding. But Oneida was flexible. Two members, Sewell Newhouse and John R. Miller, persuaded the community to begin small manufacturing. Perfectionism, they claimed, could be practiced within the American economy. The four major industries—steel animal traps, traveling bags, preserved fruit, and silk thread—enabled Oneida to create a solid economic basis, and by 1857 Oneida was showing a profit. Making money for its own sake was frowned upon, but with the economic profits the community allowed itself a few luxuries such as musical instruments and a library. Communal economics likened the ideal employer–employee relationship to that of a family. There would be a community of interest as each would be an interested partner in the business. The family relationship, then, would be one of mutual aid and liking.

The Oneida Association also regarded itself as a "school" whose object was the financial support of the community, and the spiritual support of its members' bodies and souls. Daily routines were considered a part of the total education of man. The members were to strive for "peace and fellowship; to please Christ by putting away all laziness and shiftlessness; and to assert and maintain the supremacy of spiritual interests, not allowing business to crowd these interests" (Robertson 1970:212).

The people of Oneida were industrious workers. Their products became well known for their excellent quality. By 1868 Oneida had adopted a flexible attitude toward economic processes and development; they experimented with many new endeavors and phased out the less profitable ventures. Flexibility in economic production was a strong factor in their viability, allowing them to apply the Perfectionist doctrine and to combine modern technological equipment and techniques with moneymaking ventures. With the increase of prosperity, Oneida began to hire outside labor not only in industries but also in their household, laundry, and kitchen. They paid attractive wages and treated their employees well.

Self-enrichment was encouraged by a balance of work and leisure. Games were very popular at Oneida. (Photo courtesy of Oneida, Ltd.)

SOCIAL PATTERNS: EQUALITY, AFFECTION,
AND COMPLEX MARRIAGE

Life at Oneida was operated on a balance of work and leisure, practicality and self-enrichment. After the community was economically secure, members permitted themselves many luxuries for their enjoyment. Because Perfectionism placed great emphasis on education for self-improvement, the library in the Mansion House was well equipped with books of all sorts. Interests in art, music, and literature were encouraged. This strong emphasis on cultivation through leisure was balanced by the pervasive practicality of the group. The dress patterns of the women were adapted for utility and freedom of movement; women's dresses were shortened, pantalets (loose trousers) were worn, and their hair was worn short.

The work patterns of the Oneida members followed practical rules. Members awoke when they would, ate only two meals a day (mostly cold and vegetarian foods), and claimed to have few rules about the hours required for working. Calling both wasteful, Noyes argued against a three-meal day and hot animal foods. He considered work to be a healthy endeavor—unless it was overdone—and

By working in "bees," labor was made into a sport. This group is shown making traveling bags. (Photograph before 1868, courtesy of Oneida, Ltd.)

to ensure against this distinct possibility, he wanted to reduce the work day from eight to six hours. The work system was based on rotation of tasks, and much work resembled play by the initiation of work "bees" to speed it and give some sport to it. His ideal was to focus on efficiency of production, distribution, and organization. To this end he relied on the spirit of brotherhood and love of his community members. Strict reproach was sometimes needed, however, for laziness or delinquency would bring severe criticism.

The hardheaded, practical men who ran the community businesses were more realistic than Noyes. For example, young men were expected to volunteer to milk the cows early in the morning. Men were sent outside to acquire professional training for skills they needed.

Recreation at Oneida was well planned and considered important. Music and dancing were important pursuits for everyone, and Oneida had an orchestra and many instrumentalists. All forms of games such as croquet, hiking, chess, and dominoes were held in high esteem. Community activities provided a balance between coordinated activities such as marching, and competitive ones such as baseball. The members appeared to be able to demonstrate this balance in their leisure activities and to work together successfully on economic enterprises as well.

All members were allowed and often were expected to vary their residence between Oneida and Wallingford, the most successful of five small branch communities. These changes of environment were advocated as a positive step in eliminating routine and boredom. Because of their close ties in leadership and economic patterns the two communities were virtually inseparable.

The most important social feature of a day at Oneida was the evening meeting. These hour-long informal gatherings included all adults. They discussed business, religion, current events, common interests, and heard home talks by Noyes. These discussions had a moderator, but any member could participate. The meetings gave members the feeling of involvement with the workings of the community.

Ideally, all community members including men and women were equal before God. In practice and by the feminist standards of today, they were not equal. In referring to the "ascending fellowship," Noyes himself said, "in the fellowship between man and woman, for instance, man is naturally the superior" (Carden 1969:67). He wrote of women as having very different qualities, temperament, and capacities compared to men. In line with this belief, most household work, cleaning, sewing, and mending was done by women. Men ran the businesses. Men could suggest sexual encounters and women could (in theory) accept or refuse. Women, nonetheless, did work in the factory, help in the canning business, work in the silk business, and receive an education similar though not identical to men's. Women were, however, more "equal" than were women outside Oneida, and were less oppressed with childbearing, child care, and subjection to male whims.

The relatively high regard for women was compatible with the unique system of Complex Marriage developed by Noyes. In writing to a male follower he reflected its religious rationale: "I call a certain woman my wife. She is yours, she is Christ's, and in Him she is the bride of all saints" (Carden 1969:8). In 1838 Noyes married Harriet Holton. Of the five children Harriet bore, four were still-

The bobbed hair, short skirts, and pantalets of the women created much comment by outsiders. (Photo courtesy of Oneida, Ltd.)

born. Noyes came to the conclusion that childbearing was physically and mentally hard on women, and he therefore advocated "intelligent well-ordered procreation," that is, propagation not tied to the expression of emotions.

Noyes likened Perfectionism to Heaven, and as there was no marriage in Heaven, there would be no marriage in his system. As all men were past death and sin, they would follow Christ and Paul, who said that marriage also would be done away with. "The new commandment is that we love one another and that not by pairs, as in the world, but en masse. The restoration of the true relations between the sexes is a matter second in importance only to the reconciliation of man to God" (Robertson 1970:267). In this system, love relationships were not restricted to couples, for all members of the community were expected to love one another. Monogamy was regarded by Noyes as "a form of spiritual tyranny" in which men and women have unwarranted power over each other based on religious rules rather than love (Lockwood 1965:191). Just as all property was shared communally, so should all people. Free cohabitation was to pervade all of life and not be stifled by a restrictive relationship. In practice, however, the system was hedged about with restrictions for both men and women. A careful check was kept on who had (and who could have) sexual relations with whom—in keeping with the rule of ascending fellowship.[1]

[1] The idea of ascending fellowship was that people ought to associate with those others in the community who were at a higher level of spiritual growth than themselves in order to absorb some of the good spiritual qualities of others. There was no danger to the more advanced person in the reverse process.

In this system the burden of chastity no longer belonged solely to women, for both partners became equally responsible for the act of love. Such ideas resulted in the unique community form of birth control, male continence, and the experiment in scientific propagation, which Noyes termed Stiripculture. This carefully engineered plan symbolized for Noyes the "highest and most sacred art that humans could cultivate," and was a path to perfection through selective breeding (Parker 1935:257). Noyes believed that by scientific propagation good physical and spiritual qualities could be bred into humans in the same manner in which cattle were selectively bred. As motherhood was not the sole object of womanhood in the community, all women were not obliged to give birth. Although each member had sexual relations with many other members, reproduction was selective and required the approval of the central members. This was achieved through stiripculture, which classified the sexual act in three stages: (1) the simple presence of the organ, (2) motion, and (3) ejaculation. Men were to stop at Stage 1 or Stage 2, but never to complete Stage 3. Amative intercourse, stopping at Stage 1 or 2, was viewed as spiritual, pleasurable, and satisfying in itself. It was a form of art in which the union of persons provided an interchange of great spiritual depth.

Although Noyes had been committed in principle long before his marriage, the actual workings of the system of complex marriage and stiripculture began in Putney when Noyes was attracted to a woman other than his wife. After this woman, Mary Cragin, became his sexual partner the central members of the community started the practice. At Oneida, the procedure was somewhat formalized. A sexual contact was usually conducted through a third party. The male would initiate the request to a woman through an older woman. In theory any woman could refuse or accept without embarrassment.[2] Exclusive attachments between specific couples were frowned upon, and any couple that developed an exclusive relationship was sanctioned with the help of a third party (and almost everyone else) who prevented secret meetings and broke up the exclusive love attachment. One's responsibility was to the entire community, and therefore singular love became dysfunctional for the entire system.

From 1849 to 1869 the "Community had deliberately refrained from bringing children into the world, [by] increasing its number less than two a year in a population of some forty families. Like all prudent parents, the Community awaited 'responsible maturity and favorable circumstances'" (Parker 1935:256). After twenty years of testing the practicability of its sexual principles, the community was ready in 1869 to enter the stage of "scientific propagation" that they called stiripculture. All consenting members were to sign a contract with the community. Fifty-three women (probably all of childbearing age) signed the following resolutions:

[2] On this point, Maren Lockwood Carden, an expert on Oneida, wrote to the senior author (1973): "I do not believe this oft-repeated propaganda. See the van de Walker article [cf. biblio. in Carden 1969:215, 216] for some evidence to the contrary. Also the *Daily Record*. In my judgement the third party (usually an older woman) "told" the women whether they ought to accept or not. That way the central members controlled the whole sexual system."

1. That we do not belong to ourselves in any respect, but that we do belong first to God, and second to Mr. Noyes as God's true representative.
2. That we have no rights or personal feelings in regard to child-bearing which shall in the least degree oppose or embarrass him in his choice of scientific combinations.
3. That we will put aside all envy, childishness, and selfseeking, and rejoice with those who are chosen candidates; that we will, if necessary, become martyrs to science, and cheerfully resign all desire to become mothers, if for any reason Mr. Noyes deem us unfit material for propagation. Above all, we offer ourselves living sacrifices to God and true Communism (Parker 1935:257).

Thirty-eight men in the community signed a corresponding statement, which was given to Noyes:

The undersigned desire you may feel that we most heartily sympathize with your purpose in regard to scientific propagation, and offer ourselves to be used in forming any combinations that may seem to you desirable. We claim no rights. We ask no privileges. We desire to be servants of the truth. With a prayer that the Grace of God will help us in this resolution, we are your true soldiers (Parker 1935:257).

Noyes had seen the administration of stiripculture as the responsibility of the older men (he believed youth too impulsive), and a committee was formed for the selection of parents. Application was made by couples who desired to become parents. Sometimes the leaders made suggestions as to who should make application. Theodore, the oldest son of the founder, for example, felt obligated to father children when he really did not want to. Members knew their relative standing in the community only too well. Those who wanted children but who knew that their application would be rejected probably did not bother making formal application (Carden 1973, personal correspondence).

Since the quality of each child was thought to depend more upon the man's character than the woman's, the males was subjected to more scrutiny than the female. In the ten years of the experiment (1869–1879), 9 applications were rejected, 42 couples were mated, and 52 children (or stiripcults) were born, 4 of these being stillbirths. Thirteen of the 52 children were unplanned. Noyes himself was the father of 9 children and 1 stillbirth in Oneida's eugenics experiment.

Once the children were born, they were to be children of the community. Parents were expected to focus on the spiritual welfare of their children to please God. Members believed that exclusive devotion to the rearing of children was not enough for one's own spiritual well-being. The system of child rearing, therefore, was carried out in the Children's Wing of the Mansion House, where the child was not dependent solely on parental attention. The mother cared for the child until weaning (about nine months), when the child proceeded to the first department of the Children's Wing. There the child stayed from eight to five o'clock and was cared for by nurses. At about one-and-a-half years old, the child entered the second department, where he stayed all day. Parents were permitted to visit, but at this period they gradually gave up responsibility for the child and were free to rejoin the work force. At three years old, the child entered the third department, where he stayed until he was about fourteen years old. There were special efforts to "communize the children." All toys and playthings were held in common. Children were taught in formal classes and encouraged to read widely in the community library. They were taught to be spiritual, and great emphasis was placed on religious teachings. The community itself was thought to be the best possible school for learning the ways of Perfectionism, although the children did have formal religious lessons. Boys of twelve to seventeen years old were given various jobs around the community, while girls of ten to twelve years old were given household duties. In times of financial trouble (the 1850s), all capable children were given work duties in addition to their studies. Parents who joined Oneida brought their children with them. The children were loved, but were not seen as the main focus of community cohesion.

The community recognized the need for skilled professions and knew that, of itself, their school was insufficient. Such resources were limited, and they acknowledged it.

Through education, they desired to master the discoveries and knowledge of the outside world in order to solve its problems in their own setting. To this end, the community sent some people outside for training as physicians and other professionals.

The strength of Oneida was in its daily life, which was permeated by religion. There were no regular meetings for prayers or ritual religious practices. Although they read the Bible and quoted it frequently, there were no patterned prayers. Sunday was a day off from work for convenience but was not considered a holy day. Baptism was considered unnecessary, and death was taken lightly because as Perfectionists they believed that "life after death is very similar to life on earth" (Carden 1969:45). Their daily meetings were the institutional activity closest to organized religion, including Noyes' home talks and the confessions of members. But even these meetings were casual and included business and social discussions.

While Oneida could be at peace with itself, it couldn't prevent flare-ups with the surrounding countryside. It was plagued by various forms of hostility. Relations with some immediate neighbors and with utopian sympathizers were good, but their deviant sexual practices evoked antagonism from the "guardians of morality" in the larger society. Children were jeered by outsiders as "bastards," and the established clergy denounced their sexual practices as "harlotry, free love, and licensed indulgence." There were legal threats against the community, and Oneida publications were viewed as shrewd proselytizing.

Oneida, on the other hand, scorned the outside world as filthy and degrading. Children were not to speak with outsiders, visitors, or persons who were employees; those who came in contact with local village boys were revolted by their swearing and foul language. After visitors left the community a "bee" was usually held to clean the quarters and eradicate any trace of impurity. In effect this was a ritual way of housecleaning. Oneida members who were about to travel underwent mutual criticism before their departure, and again on their return, to cleanse them of "spiritual contamination."

POLITY: AUTOCRACY AND MUTUAL CRITICISM

The authority system at Oneida had two divergent aspects. Despite Noyes' claim that the Christian Bible was the source of knowledge, it was his own writings and despotic rule that provided the foundation for Oneida's system of government. On the other hand, there was limited democracy through mutual criticism and through open discussion at the evening meetings.

In the early days of the community there were twenty-one standing committees and forty-eight administrative departments to operate the daily workings of the group. The yearly appointments to committees were made on the basis of ability and the desire to serve. The heads of each department formed the Business Board, which met weekly. Their notes and proposals were reported at the daily meeting, where consensus would be sought to implement a new policy. Once a year each department sent a report to the Finance Committee. Along the way careful book-keeping and inventories made the system very efficient.

Noyes' role was that of overseer. He considered himself a despotic ruler, but he also convinced the members that "service was perfect freedom." He did not control all aspects of the community but outlined the general principles and left their execution to the Central Members. Always the older members of the community, these Central Members were the major voices in community affairs. They guarded the tenets of Perfectionism and were the elite of Oneida, and their position afforded them certain advantages such as travel and choice of sexual partners. The Central Member's believed that democracy at Oneida was impossible because Complex Marriage, as practiced, depended upon the rule of ascending fellowship. The duty of close regulation fell to those highest in fellowship, namely Mr. Noyes, who was believed to be divinely inspired, and the Central Members.

The other method of governance at Oneida was through sessions of mutual criticism, in which members openly discussed the virtues and faults of others. It was an extremely powerful form of social control, and members saw it as the "power which harmonizes [the Association] and constitutes its government" (Robertson 1970:134). Intended to balance man as a worker and as a spiritual being, criticism was meted out to all, although the Central Members and Noyes were treated gently. Any transgression of Perfectionist doctrine was likely to be just cause. Persons who came out of a criticism session claimed to have felt renewed, but emotionally drained. The method was also used somewhat unsuccessfully to try to cure physical illnesses that were believed to be the result of a weak moral and spiritual composition. They later resorted to conventional medicine as an additional source of medical care.

THE DECLINE OF ONEIDA

The decline of Oneida resulted more from internal conflict than from external stress. The neighbors at Oneida tolerated the community's strange form of social life and actually believed that it was an asset because of its many business interests. However, both internal and external pressure did have an effect on its demise.

Several factors were responsible for Oneida's deterioration. Lack of commitment to the religious principles weakened the community. This was also indicative in the new generation of members who were born in the community. The children had always played competitive, noncooperative games, which led to a spirit of rivalry; the natural step was one very much against communal ideas of sharing and loving. In addition children had been encouraged to read and learn of the outside world, giving them a knowledge that could only disrupt the community's way of life. While the lack of religious commitment weakened the community, it was the internal events of 1876 to 1880 that finally brought its demise (Robertson 1972:262–279).

Noyes attempted to transfer the leadership of the community to his eldest son, Theodore Noyes, an agnostic, in 1876. Other, younger sons were unsuited, for the stiripcults were less than six years old, and Noyes' other son, Victor Cragin Noyes (born of Mary Cragin about 1847) had spent time in a local insane asylum. Theodore Noyes remained aloof from the community but instilled regimentation. Serious internal troubles arose over the way Oneida was being governed so that the elder Noyes was forced to return from retirement at Wallingford to re-establish his position. But the rebellion continued, this time centering on John Humphrey Noyes himself. A crisis raged over who would initiate the young virgins (often twelve or thirteen years old) into the complex-marriage system. Noyes had always been the first husband, and once Noyes' rule was questioned there was much opposition (Carden 1969:100). Two factions arose—the Noyesites and the Townerites (after James Towner, the chief opponent of Noyes). While the community was still in an uproar about this issue, charges of statutory rape and adultery were brought against Noyes. Meanwhile the community members themselves were charging him with despotism.

Noyes left the community in June of 1876 for Canada. In his absence, the community agreed to continue complex marriage, and they chose new ground rules that were amenable to both sides. The new Council that was appointed to manage the system began to have problems. They sent word to Noyes in Niagara Falls requesting advice, and in August of 1879, Noyes sent back proposals to abandon the system of complex marriage. The community accepted his proposals, and stated that by a unanimous vote they gave up the practice of complex marriage, "not as renouncing belief in the principles and prospective finality of the institution, but in deference to the public sentiment which is evidently rising against it" (Holloway 1966:195). Similarly, joint housekeeping and communal sharing were abandoned because they could no longer make them work. The new arrangement included two classes of people, marrieds and celibates. Members were advised to choose the celibate path, but most chose to get married.

In 1881 the Oneida Community was re-organized into the Oneida Community, Limited, a joint-stock corporation. Most analysts hold this to be the end of the utopian phase of the Oneida Community. Eighty-five descendants of the original Perfectionists still lived in the immediate area in 1962. Today the company continues to manufacture silverware and in recent years has offered the sale of stock to the public. The vision of perfection on earth dissolved into a thriving capitalistic enterprise.

4

The Hutterites:
The Christian Bruderhof

The Hutterian Brethren are the oldest, the largest, and the most thriving of all communal societies in North America. They are traditional, German-speaking Christians who have survived the persecutions of the Reformation, the Thirty Years' War, the efforts of the Hapsburg Empire and the Jesuits to convert them back to Catholicism, the nationalizing influence of Russia, and the wartime patriotism of the United States and Canada. Twice in their history, communal living was abandoned, but each time it was revived. When they came to South Dakota from the Ukraine in 1874 they numbered about 400 persons in three colonies. Today in the northwestern plains area there are over 220 agricultural colonies, with a population of over 22,000, numbering about a hundred to a colony.

The data for this study is based on the findings of an extensive research effort and reported in *The Hutterites in North America* (Hostetler and Huntington 1967), a Case Study in Cultural Anthropology.

ORIGIN: A COUNTERCULTURE IN A TOTALITARIAN EMPIRE

Originating in the Austrian Tyrol and Moravia during the Protestant Reformation in the sixteenth century, the Hutterites are one of three surviving Anabaptist groups. The Anabaptists were religiously based counterculture groups who rejected infant baptism and membership in state churches. The Hutterites were not simply negatively oriented by refusing infant baptism and by repudiating membership in the state churches but, in addition, formed "communities of love" (Troeltsch 1931:331–334). Private property was to be abolished, possessions were to be surrendered voluntarily by the individual, and through Christian pacifism wars were to come to an end. Their position was viewed as heretical and socially revolutionary by both state and church authorities.

The practice of "community of goods" was instituted in 1528 while a group of believing Anabaptists in distress was traveling from Nikolsburg to Austerlitz (today in Czechoslovakia). Thus what had been done out of expediency was incorporated as a major belief. The first Bruderhof, a self-sustaining colony of people involved in communal living (literally, a "brother household"), was founded

34

in Austerlitz in Moravia. Jacob Hutter of Tyrol joined the community and greatly intensified the discipline of rigorous communal living. He was captured by the authorities, interrogated, brutally whipped, and burned at the stake in 1536. Although not the founder of the Hutterites, who are named after him, Hutter was their most outstanding organizer and leader.

For two generations the Hutterites were protected from the Hapsburg government by local barons of Moravia who found them to be outstanding farmers and craftsmen. In this short time they prospered, expanding to approximately eighty well-managed colonies with an estimated population of over 20,000 persons.

With the outbreak of war between Austria and Turkey in 1593 the Hutterites were systematically crushed by heavy taxation, plundering, and torture. Many were executed or sent into captivity. The disastrous Thirty Years' War followed, and by 1622 all the Hutterites had been driven from Moravia. In Hungary and in several small states to the east, they rebuilt their communities only to deteriorate and suffer concerted pressures from the Jesuits, under which many accepted Catholicism. In 1767 a remnant crossed the Carpathian mountains into Wallachia, where they were soon caught in the Russo-Turkish War. On invitation from a Russian general, less than a hundred Hutterites settled in the Ukraine in 1770.

Here the Hutterites were granted complete religious freedom, exemption from military duty, and free practice of their trades. Upon achieving reasonable material recovery after so many years of hardship, a period of decline set in. Communal ownership was abandoned from 1819 to 1859. An extensive religious revival of communal living began in 1856, and in 1859 communal living was restored. Scarcely had the group reinstituted communal living when the Russian government changed its attitude toward German colonists: With large numbers of unassimilated Germans living on choice lands in the Ukraine, a new nationalization policy was instituted. The Hutterites, along with many Mennonites, Doukhobors, and other minorities, then migrated to North America. The entire Hutterite population, numbering nearly 800 persons, relocated in South Dakota. The three colonies founded in South Dakota (1874–1877) are the progenitors of three separate affiliations (Leut) of Hutterites.

IDEOLOGY: COMMUNAL LIVING, THE WAY TO PARADISE

The Hutterites derive their beliefs from the Hebrew-Christian Bible and from the Apocrypha. Many are similar to those of other Christian groups, yet they differ sharply in their application. More than the Family and the Oneida group, the Hutterites have had a long historical span over which to develop their beliefs. The resulting complex social system allows organized patterns of interaction, both within the Hutterite community and between the Hutterites and outside society.

Hutterites believe that absolute authority resides in a single omnipotent God, Who created the universe and placed everything in a divine and hierarchical order. All that is of God is considered to be spiritual, unchanging, and eternal, while all that is classed as material or created is conceived as temporal, changing, and

View of a Hutterite colony half-hidden in a ravine along the Saskatchewan River.

transitory. This respect for the right or divine order, which requires a hierarchy of relationships, pervades Hutterite action and thought in everyday affairs. The superior cares for, directs, and uses the subordinate; the subordinate serves and obeys the superior. God is Lord over man, man is master of woman, and the older person has authority over the younger. Humans have power over animals and are "lord of the same." Human beings may rule over material things, inventions, and machines, and use them as long as the proper relation and function are observed. Humans may not change the order of God (e.g., kill other humans) or interfere with the process of natural conception.

This concept of divine order is, therefore, a tenet of the Hutterites. Marital relations are governed by it also. God rules over the soul or spirit, the spirit rules over the body, and man rules over woman. Man has lordship over woman, who is characterized by weakness, humility, and submission. Man "should have compassion on the woman as the weaker instrument" and must care for her in temporal and spiritual things. From the beginning God ordained all things for proper function and for common use. Through disobedience, however, man brought disorder into the world. By his grasping and greedy spirit man has made private possession of the things of God. Carnal or unbelieving persons are viewed as living in perpetual covetousness by making property, food, land, and "created things" the objects of private gain.

Community (*Gemeinschaft*) in the Hutterite view means a group of members of the Church who are united in the fellowship of the Holy Spirit under the leadership of the spirit of Christ. This group is called "the community of the Church of Christ," "the communion of saints," and "the children of God," and is conceived

Center square of a Hutterite colony. The church is in the middle, surrounded by traditional longhouses, older dwellings, and communal kitchen.

as a foretaste (*Vorhof*) of life after death. A notion rejected by the Hutterites is that of the purely "spiritual" community that does not bring property under the control of the body of Christ.

The ideology of the Hutterites is, therefore, reflected in the social organization and in the lifeways of the people. Just as man must surrender to the will of God, so also must the individual submit to the will of the community, where all material and spiritual gifts are shared and held in common. These basic beliefs become the reference points that color the group's view of reality.

SUBSISTENCE: WORK AND ECONOMIC ACTIVITY

Hutterites are agriculturalists. Many are located in dry land farming areas, but because of past restrictions against communal ownership of land in some areas, many colonies do not own the best lands. With good management, rotation of crops, and use of fertilizers, arable lands produce modest-to-good grain yields. Nonarable land is good pasture. Depending upon the productivity of the soil, colonies own or rent from 4000 to 16,000 acres, on which are raised cattle, sheep, hogs, poultry, and dairy herds.

A Hutterite colony is a community of work. All persons are required to work according to their ability, and the professed purpose of labor is that the needs of all may be supplied. The productive capacity of a colony varies with the size of its population, acreage, and the number of adults in the labor force. The productive strategy is to maintain a wide diversity of agricultural enterprises so there will be work for everyone throughout the year. The various enterprises are carefully reviewed by the colony yearly. Important factors entering into decision making for the productive enterprises are the growth of the colony population, the degree of mechanization they can afford, the capability of the person in charge of a given enterprise, and the ability of the group to arrive at an amicable consensus. Since consensus is more important for "the good of the colony" than sheer efficiency, the Hutterites have refrained generally from speculative production. A large volume with a small but steady profit is considered more important than enterprises yielding the largest margin of profit.

A significant part of the yearly work strategy depends on a dynamic pattern integrated with the seasons, for lack of work could mean the breakdown of a smooth-running colony. In summer there is a greater need for labor than in winter. During the winter months the colony absorbs the additional labor by reassigning jobs and by giving each department additional younger apprentices. In winter the gardener becomes a carpenter, and the preacher who looks after the geese in summer concentrates on bookbinding. The carpenter has two extra helpers in winter for making household furniture, and the shop mechanic has additional help for overhauling machinery. The pigman has an extra boy assigned to him.

Competition between department managers proves to be healthy for the welfare of the colony, for it does not involve direct competition between individuals or their assigned status. Rather, it is between income-producing phases of the operations. Modern technical knowledge is borrowed and used from outside the colony.

Author John Hostetler hoeing with colony members. (Photo by National Film Board of Canada.)

All Hutterite colonies are basically alike in their social organization and expansion characteristics. Eventually, each colony comes to form its own new colony by a planned method called "branching out," a fission made necessary by population growth. This requires careful management of capital assets and investments; redistribution of colony authority; consideration of family and kinship factors; and the designing of new work patterns. The growth span between branchings varies, but the average is about fourteen years. During this time a colony may increase from about 70 to 130 persons. When a colony reaches a maximal population size (130–150 persons), members begin to sense management problems—problems of affluence, inefficiency, and supervision.

The growth of a colony is marked by successive stages from the time it is formed until it produces a daughter colony. The parent colony is usually responsible for 50 percent of the small colony's debts, and this new colony must work hard to pay off the other half. The reason behind this is that a debt-free colony, now in its second stage, will expand its land holdings and obtain more equipment to provide more jobs for its growing population. A third stage follows, the period of affluence when a colony is able to save money for expansion, to loan money to other needy colonies, and to make and install laborsaving devices.

Division of certain kinds of equipment between the newly formed colony and the mother colony is decided by lot. The lot also determines which of two groups must move to the new colony. The preacher, with the aid of his assistant, lists families on the blackboard in two groups, each of which is headed by the name of one of the preachers. Family heads are permitted to choose between the two preachers. Older people are grouped according to their known preferences, but a balance between the two groups is worked out that takes into account age, sex, family size, and relatedness.

The process of branching is supported by strong authority patterns, and its highest ideal is impartiality, involving both persons and property. Only the will of God is strong enough to separate family members and to break personal, sentimental ties. Individual desires must be subordinated to the will of the community, through which the will of God is manifested.

The concept of personal property to an adult Hutterite means the right to use but not to possess. Considered as personal property are those items that have been formally given to the individual by the colony, plus anything acquired by the individual with money from his small allowance. Such belongings are kept in a chest under lock and key. Personal belongings are passed on to the children and sometimes to other relatives before or after the individual dies. Yardgoods that have not been utilized for clothing are returned to the colony storehouse at the time of death. Ideally all personal gifts from neighbors or outsiders are reported to the householder. In practice, however, individuals are permitted to keep some of these gifts they may have earned in return for work or favors. Some of these gifts, such as binoculars for sheepherding, benefit the colony.

From the viewpoint of children growing up in a colony there are two kinds of property: things under lock and key, to which access is forbidden, and material that is not locked up. The latter is accessible and available for use. The practice of using padlocks in the colony is followed under the widespread expectation that children will get into everything.

The distribution pattern of goods reflects colony conceptions of impartiality and equality in sharing. The amount and kind of goods, determined by the rules of the intercolony association, are distributed according to individual need as defined by Hutterite values. The society is not only communal in production, but also in its consumption and distribution phases: Food is consumed in a communal setting, and clothing and most other essentials are distributed through resident household units. Although the society is communal and modern in its technology and productive features, its adherence to religious authority prevents a distributive economy based on the maximization of the individual wants. Profits realized from the marketplace are held by the corporation for the welfare of the whole colony.

SOCIAL PATTERNS: FAMILY, PEER GROUP, AND COMMUNAL CONTENTMENT

The average Hutterite colony consists of four longhouses, with four families in each longhouse. Built on a sixteenth century floor plan, longhouses are usually 100 feet long and 36 feet wide running north and south, with four entrances. Each family lives together in an apartment consisting of a middle room and two bed-rooms associated with each entrance. From the middle room stairs go to the attic, which is often one large room in which all the families in that longhouse store their out-of-season clothing and furniture. When a couple marries they are given a room and if possible an entrance of their own. As their family increases they are given additional rooms. The apartment is the center of the universe for the child under two and a half or three, but for the older members it is primarily a place to sleep and to store things. Food preparation takes place in the central kitchen, outside the longhouse, and all meals are eaten in the colony's central dining room. Clothes are washed in the colony laundry, and baths are taken in the colony bathhouse.

There is little privacy. Children run around in the attic and into one another's apartments through the attic entrance. Colony people do not knock when they visit one another, nor do they hesitate to enter if no one is home. Not only is privacy de-emphasized, but the constant surveillance in the colony is actually valued.

The function of the family is to produce new souls and to care for them until the colony gradually takes over the major responsibility of training the children around age three. The family performs those functions that cannot easily or efficiently be performed by the colony. Children are not thought of as a form of private enterprise or as an extension of the parents' egos, but as gifts of God who belong to the colony and potentially to the Church. Viewed as such, the community has placed no limit to the number of children a couple may have, and birth-

Hutterite married couple and some of their children.

control practices are forbidden. The median size of the completed family is about ten children. The median age at marriage for women is 22.0 and for men 23.5, and only 1.9 percent of the men and 5.4 percent of the women over age 30 had never married, as reported by Eaton and Mayer (1954). There is a strong but heeded prohibition of sexual relations before marriage, and only one divorce and four desertions have occurred in a century.

Intrafamily relationships with parents, siblings, grandparents, uncles, aunts, and cousins are of primary importance to the individual throughout his life. Hutterites say *Blut ist kein Wasser*, meaning blood ties are not to be taken lightly. In line with the dichotomy between male and female subcultures, women feel closer to the mother's relatives, especially the mother's sisters, than to the relatives of their father. The reverse holds true for the men.

The Hutterite colony functions in many ways as an extended family, for all are committed to the principle of spiritual brother- and sisterhood. Because Hutterite society has institutionalized a continuing relationship between parents and children, the family is emotionally less demanding and exclusive than is the rule in middle-class American society.

The human life span is patterned into age categories: house children, kindergartners, school children, young people, baptism, marriage and adulthood, and the old people. A highly effective system of education characterizes the earlier years, but does not stop at a certain age. The major levels of formal education are kindergarten (*Klein-Schul*), German school (*Gross-Schul*), Sunday school

Hutterite children eat in their own dining room and work under the supervision of a teacher.

(*Suntag-Schul* or *Kinder-Schul*), baptismal instruction, and the daily evening sermons (*Gebet*). The kindergarten weans the child from his parents, teaches him to respect authority, to function in a group, and to learn the approved forms of cooperation. At every stage in life the individual is subservient to the colony and he is a member of a peer group. This group is of supreme importance, for it provides a reference group for the individual and can also punish him.

School-age children spend most of their day under close supervision of someone in authority—the teacher, parent, or work supervisor. Groups of brothers and sisters learn to work together, for this sort of interaction will continue into adulthood. Children are taught unquestioned obedience to Hutterite authority—to parents, teachers, older Hutterites, and to traditions and teachings. If they disobey they are taught to accept punishment meekly. Typically they are not instructed in self-discipline or the means to decide what is right and wrong for themselves. Rather they are taught to do what they are told and to be dependent upon the protecting care of the colony. The Hutterite appraisal of natural order is evident here, for the child has his place and must be tutored. A child's nature is regarded as carnal (selfish) and must be supplanted by the spiritual (selfless), expressed in

Hutterite schoolchildren. (Photo by Clarence Strang.)

terms of moral obligations within a social hierarchy. The Hutterites regard the child's personality as intrinsically good only as he (behaviorally) gives up his individual will and conforms voluntarily to the will of the colony. This appraisal of human nature for delinquent individuals is somewhat opposed to that of contemporary society in North America, for when a Hutterite youth transgresses the rules, he will be punished but not because he was bad. The adolescent who occasionally transgresses the rules can still see himself as being on the road toward goodness. Since the colony knows everyone is bad from the start, the wrongdoer must suffer the consequences of his behavior. Natural badness is only temporary and will, with maturity, be supplanted by responsibility. Hutterite society makes it a point to forgive when true signs of betterment are observed. These manifestations are encouraged and rewarded. When the individual becomes a full member, he is obligated to teach and uphold the morality of his society.

The expectations for the individual within the social structure are clearly defined by the ideology and are reinforced by the social patterns. Each individual knows what is expected of him, wants to act in keeping with them, and, in most instances, is able to do so. The individual is never asked to mortify the basic human drives but, rather, to subject them to a community of love that is both human and divine. A matter as difficult as sex is managed in such a way that it is not a threat to reproductive patterns, as with some communal Christian groups. Relations are restricted to married pairs, and there is no evidence of any tendency toward celibacy or continence after marriage.

Modern Hutterite dwelling with living units for four families.

While the individual submits to the community will, he is offered security and social support in exchange. Families are generally happy and supportive of the colony's superior power position, and the Hutterite may reflect an attitude that appears to the outsider as egocentrism or pride. However, he is not expressing personal pride but simply a state of mind that has no doubts about a way of life. The emotional identification with the colony is evidenced by the number who return after "trying the world" and by the relatively few who permanently desert the colony.

POLITY: THEISTIC AUTHORITY AND HUMAN CONSENSUS

Hutterite policy and leadership within the colony combine the authority of the supernatural with human consensus. Many of their problems are solved by a long tradition arrived at by trial and error, and by a system of absolutism whose firm notions of morality are shared by all. The concept of "sacred time," for example, influences the behavior patterns and the social organization of the colony. While this perspective relates to creation and the eternal, "secular time" is the mere measure of earthly events and applies to all material objects including the human body.

All authority both inside and outside the Church is believed to originate with God. Governmental authority and police power is ordained by God to maintain order among the godless. Within the Church, however, there is order without physical coercion. Composed of all the baptized members of the colony, the Church as a group, not as individuals, has the power to accept and to exclude members. Because woman is "the weaker instrument," her place is necessarily subordinate. Women participate in the church service by being present, by joining in the prayers and hymns, and by formally greeting newly baptized members, but they do not participate in formulating colony policy. They are not eligible for church leadership or colony departmental positions such as cattleman, shop mechanic, and shoemaker. Only baptized men can vote to elect members to these positions or decide the economic, social, and religious life of the colony.

Each colony has a council that functions as an executive committee, making decisions such as who shall be allowed to go to town or to visit relatives. Five to seven baptized men serve as council members, who initiate changes in the appointment of departmental and subordinate positions, execute discipline, and perform judicial functions. Council members hold the key positions in the colony, including those of First Preacher, Second Preacher, Householder, and Field Manager. Often the German-school teacher and one or two other men who hold leadership positions in the colony or whose age entitles them to a position of authority are elected to the council. Although the First Preacher has the highest leadership position, his actions are subject to review by the council. Authority is thus group-centered, and decisions are derived through unified and continuous decision making by the council members.

Within the Hutterite colony two sometimes opposing subcultures exist, that of the men and that of the women. Women are believed to be inferior to men intellectually and physically and to need direction, protection, guidance, and consideration. Although women as a group do not participate in formal colony decisions, they are relatively free to intervene when they or their families are affected. They may never defend their position on the basis of being an individual, but must appeal to the welfare of the group. Women, as a group, support each other against masculine influence.

Nonetheless, certain women have nonrotating positions of responsibility assigned to them. The most influential is that of Head Cook, and the second most influential is that of Gardener. The Tailoress is frequently the oldest active woman in the colony, and with the help of one or two elderly women, she divides the cloth and distributes clothing and tools among the colony members, keeping a record of what has been distributed. Generally two older or unmarried women are assigned to care for the kindergarten. The women alternate and are in charge of the kindergarten for one day at a time.

Despite the status distinctions and problems of Hutterite life, all come together at the daily service of worship, which integrates all of life—work, time, authority, the mundane, and the unusual. The tempo of the service is restful and unhurried, indicating an awareness of sacred time. The hymns are sung slowly, the minister reads the sermon in a stylized chant, and the prayer is long and recited softly. The community symbolically returns to the time of its origins—to Jacob Hutter, the twelve Apostles, and the spiritual source of its power—so that it may recreate its existence beyond secular time. Performing both a ritual and a didactic function, the service serves as the occasion for instruction in discipline, faith, history, and the reason for existence. It is followed immediately by a community meal, in which temporal bread immediately follows spiritual sustenance.

The church service reinforces the basic pattern of Hutterite life and simultaneously gives relief and depth by differentiating the sacred from the secular, thus permitting behavior and responses on a different plane. Within the service—protected, surrounded, and observed by every other colony member—life becomes predictable, time is no longer fleeting, each individual is essential, and women may raise their voices in singing above those of the men. The words of the sermon are believed to flow from and to remain part of God, as it reinforces the values the full members have internalized. The church gathering is the highest moment of integration in the life of the community; it encompasses and gives meaning to all of life.

5

Comparisons and Implications

When a physical scientist undertakes an investigation, he follows a fairly routine procedure. In his specialized laboratory he isolates phenomena, determines their functional elements, and subjects them to a variety of tests. These tests, using sophisticated equipment, measure the behavior of the phenomena in unusual or extreme stresses and settings. By manipulating his subject the physical scientist makes his discoveries.

In the study of man and culture, however, the anthropologist has no such specialized laboratory. For when human culture is manipulated or studied out of its natural setting, the very nature of the subject changes. Perhaps the first great lesson learned by anthropology was that man, culture, and environment are interdependent—one cannot be changed without changing the others. This means that anthropologists cannot study cultures in the comfortable setting of a scientific laboratory. Instead, we must go out into the field to observe the culture first hand. Perhaps we will see things in that culture that no one else has, or perhaps not. For it is not in the stories written about individual cultures (ethnographies) that anthropology lays claim to being a science. It is in the comparison of cultures which can be systematically contrasted that anthropological theory is based.

The three groups cited in this Basic Unit provide several bases for comparison. All three are called communal or communitarian societies, the implication being that they share a similar economic structure. They hold that the benefits of production should be equally distributed to all members of the group. The economic structure, it is theorized, is thus one of the basic variables on which societies may be compared. Are there any other features of communal societies that are constant? For instance, will communal societies all share similar kinship systems or polity structures? If we discover that communal societies do indeed have more similarities than simply the one aspect of their economic profile, we might propose some tentative theories about the nature of these groups. This would allow other anthropologists both to use our theories in the field and to test them in a wider range of situations than we have accounted for in this short book. They will undoubtedly discover certain limitations in the theory, and either refine it or replace it with a new theory. In this manner, anthropologists compensate for the lack of a "scientific laboratory" and learn to use the natural laboratory of societies themselves to learn about the nature of man and culture.

As a holistic and people-centered discipline, anthropology allows for the uniquenesses of personalities such as innovators and deviants, as well as the structured behavioral patterns of cultural (and symbolic) systems. For a long time anthropologists have been engaged in observing and recording data on many small societies in all parts of the world before they disappear as the result of either warfare, genocide, forced change, or assimilation. Today, however, a change is taking place as anthropologists turn their attention to the emergence of new social groupings and cultures that have not had a long tradition. All of this activity contributes toward a comparative understanding of human cultures, a characteristic that is fundamental to anthropology.

In our study we have not attempted to describe in complete detail the workings of each of the three communitarian societies. Instead, we have chosen to concentrate on a few features which might readily be compared in each. Of course, it may be that what we have chosen to ignore is more significant than what we have included. Further research will help to determine this. However, a number of comparative statements can already be made about the features we have considered in this study.

THE SETTINGS AND THE DATA

Several kinds of data are represented in the case descriptions and some information is extremely limited. Much of the data is based on historical reconstruction. Oneida is an example, being based on the observations of others, some of whom were participants in the society. Others were hostile as well as sympathetic outsiders who lived at an earlier period. In the two other studies, however, much has been learned from participant observation. The sources for the Hutterite section are based on such observation in contemporary colonies by anthropologists. A unique situation exists in that a great deal of historical data over a period of over four centuries is also available. Thus there are sufficient sources for an intensive longitudinal study of the dynamics of the group. The Family, by contrast, is based entirely on participant observation, and the data is that of a group at a given "moment" of time. There is practically no history, and there are no stabilized, intergenerational relationships as between children and grandparents. In this respect the Family is more of a cult than a culture, which by definition requires three generations to establish itself.

The three groups are in reality not sharply contrasting whole cultures, for all use the English language and are influenced by the dominant themes of western civilization. Each is a small functioning subculture having an orientation to communal living, but the three subsystems are in no sense a fair cross section of all communitarian groups. Our descriptions of them are contextual (actual events and people) and holistic in the sense of understanding interrelationships between institutions and human behavior. They are, however, three distinct phenomena, originating in different time periods. By describing their uniquenesses we have brought certain humanistic understandings into focus. If we were to seek a common denominator, to observe only their likenesses without paying attention to differences, we would be forcing the observations into a "straight jacket" and emasculating the group by doing so.

COMMUNITARIAN BUT DIVERSE

The three groups are communitarian in the sense that individual members are limited in the amount and kind of private property they control or possess exclusively. All land, earned income, and goods are owned by the corporate group. In each group, however, the individual had access to a few personal items. The Family members each had a small "stash," which tended to change from month to month. In a Hutterite colony chests were allocated to individuals for the accumulation of personal objects. In Oneida each person had his own small room.

Though it is possible to speak of these societies as communitarian in an economic sense, their differences in other respects are enormous. In their professed beliefs they are distinct and in the patterning of their human activities they are diverse. The actions members see themselves taking and their reasons for taking them differ from one group to another. What is purposeful activity to the Hutterites is repulsive to the Family members, and the reverse is equally true. Oneida and the Family were both involved in group marriage, which distinguishes them from the Hutterites. In addition, this latter group was the only community to be engaged in successful large-scale prairie agriculture.

Again it must be emphasized that each group was unique in some ways. The Family commune is in no sense to be taken as typical of communes in the modern communitarian movement. It was totally distinct from other neighboring communes in the Taos region of New Mexico and from others in the United States. Oneida was certainly not typical of nineteenth century communitarian societies, nor were the Hutterites characteristic of sixteenth century Germany! Other than common ownership of goods there is no "typical" commune social structure.

CULTURAL IDENTITY SYMBOLS

Each communitairan society is attempting to create a small world of order and tranquillity and, at the same time, to protect itself against intrusions from the outside world. A separate language is an effective cultural symbol for keeping outsiders out and for developing intimate forms of communication. Thus Family and Oneida members developed some specialized terminology. In Oneida, for example, there was stiripculture, amative intercourse, and complex marriage. Other in-group terms included "alimentiveness"—the liking for food; "principality" —a state of mind or habit, as in a drinking principality; "legal"—acting under the pressure of deity; "bee"—a system of shared work; "at-homeativeness"—comfortable or homey; and "diotriphiasis"—ego involvement or preeminence. The use of these special terms reinforces group identity. In some societies, however, the coining of words is not necessary. The Hutterites, for example, have a household language that is so different from the outsider's language that he can understand nothing unless the Hutterite will speak English.

Appearance is another outward way of showing one's distinctiveness. Oneida dress was clearly distinguishable from the dominant culture of the outside world. Because of their professed ideology of equality, the dress of the women was similar to that of men. Pantalets were devised, and the hair of women was worn short. In an attempt to dissociate themselves from hippies (another subculture, interestingly enough) the Family members cut off their beards, trimmed their hair, and dressed neatly. In addition to dress codes the Hutterites developed maximum use of language, endogamy, and geography to protect their tranquillity.

COMMITMENT MECHANISMS

Each of the communes utilizes behavioral modification processes to reduce the competitive tendencies, the idiosyncracies, and the selfish urges of the previous life style of the members. This is essential because self-sufficiency and independent thinking can be detrimental to communal goals.[1]

In the Family commune, changing the former life style was an active concern of all members. The group was highly conscious of its communal goals, self-actualization, the evolution of a "homo-gestalt," and transcendence of personality into a "unified consciousness." The initiation haircut was one of several practices required for shedding the old identity. In addition, persons were forced to give up drugs, the dress of "hip" culture, possessions, and even change their name in order to become members.

After this process, differentiating the member from the outside, the group sought to break the barriers between individuals. The Family commune used several techniques, including confrontation, for there was constant pressure to "get it on" with all the other members. Each was expected to take orders from everyone else in the group. Everyone was obligated to make things work, and when members lost sight of their goals, informal group criticism or encounter tactics was employed. If the individual was too occupied with himself, with a job, or with another person, group pressure was brought to bear upon him. The complete lack of privacy, with fifty or more people living in a single dwelling, forced individuals to change conceptions of private space. Living in close proximity was complementary to Family values, for everyone was truly aware of everyone else's business.

In the Oneida and Hutterite groups the mortification of self was clearly supported by the religious teachings. Commitment at Oneida was represented as the attempt to achieve Perfection in the form of salvation through the establishment of

[1] In an intensive study of commitment mechanisms Rosabeth Kanter (1972:75) reports that the successful nineteenth century communes tended to have "a large number of concrete social practices that helped generate and sustain the commitment of their members. They survived crises, persecution, debt, and internal dissension that proved the undoing of unsuccessful groups."

the Kingdom of God on earth. The community was essentially a school for implementing the religious philosophy. Here each member was to free himself of sin and enter into communion with God. Confession and mutual criticism, employed by many of the successful communes (Kanter 1972:106), were used to eliminate undesirable traits and to establish dependency patterns. Since democracy was believed impossible and undesirable, and members were not considered equal with respect to their spiritual development, a system of "ascending fellowship" (and resulting dependency) was important. Lesser members profited in their association with those further up on the spiritual ladder. All looked up to Central Members, and they in turn deferred to Noyes as having the final word.

Members at Oneida were further distinguishable from the dominant culture in other ways. Exclusive or individualistic relationships were tantamount to slavery, and the system of complex marriage was developed to avoid this problem. Excessive introspection and individuating tendencies were minimized by common ownership of clothing and property, by eating together, and by sharing leisure activities.

Among Hutterites there are also firm commitments from the members. The ideas of individual will and group will are significant in their opposition to each other. Even though virtually all recruits are born in the colony, the first twenty years of life are spent in learning self-surrender and obedience to God and colony. Human nature is carnal and displeasing to God. The spiritual nature can be acquired only as self-will becomes fused with the will of the community.

SOCIALIZATION

In the Family commune, socialization consisted mainly of the behavior modification of joiners. Here as in Oneida the major task was retraining adults. Unlike Oneida, however, they did not seek to perpetuate their ideals by having children or by training them properly. There were no prescribed ways, no models for child rearing. The children were individuals, had wills, and, they joked among themselves, would rebel against their parents by going to college. In fact, the oldest, a six-year-old child, was attending a local private school because the child had no play group.

Oneida made provision both for planning births and for the care of children. Though children were the property of the community, parents were expected to attend to their spiritual welfare and to support the community in their proper training. Transmitting the ways of Perfectionism was important, and this was achieved by living in the community as well as by formal instruction. Oneida was, therefore, engaged both in retraining adults who joined and in transmitting the ideals to the offspring.

In the Hutterite colonies, however, there are very few adult converts and hence no special problems in respect to absorbing the few who do join. Having probably the highest birthrate of any known society, they are concerned primarily with the proper training of their offspring. This is extremely important because more than half of the population is under fifteen years of age. They have developed a very effective means for training the young to accept the communal way of life. The continuing socialization of adults, however, is directed toward maintaining the proper social relationships and preparing the individual for death. From early childhood to old age there is uninterrupted indoctrination within clearly defined age and sex groupings. Every person is submissive to the colony at every stage of his life, and the goals for each stage are attainable by virtually all persons. Thoroughly trained to meet clearly defined roles, each member is rewarded by the awareness that his contribution is essential to the colony.

All Hutterite socialization is grounded in the supernatural, in a religiously held source of authority and absolutism that determines the proper ordering of social relationships. Children are wanted and given a great deal of attention during the first two years. In the kindergarten they are weaned from the family and learn to obey and function within their peer group.

In Hutterite society self-development is de-emphasized and individuality is subordinated to the welfare of the colony. Some informal deviancy is tolerated but kept within manageable proportions. Individual perfection is not possible, but the proper spiritual nature can be acquired with the aid of other members. The result is an emphasis on rehabilitation of the deviant individual with a minimum of condemnation.

AUTHORITY PATTERNS

Authority was made legitimate in all three groups, but power was allocated in different ways. The Hutterite community, which has survived the longest, has a highly structured decision-making process beginning with God and diffused through various levels of the community. Although ultimate decision making is isolated from the rank and file, all members are involved in the daily decisions. God, whose will is manifested through the scriptures, is considered the ultimate authority. This concept of religious supremacy is also found in Oneida and in the Family, although interpreted in a different manner. Within the Family, order is believed to flow from what the members call "Cosmic Energy." All professed beliefs and activities are linked to this source.

In all three groups supernatural authority is articulated by the leaders or spokesmen. Social distance is maintained between the ultimate decision-making process and the members, but with varying degrees of success. The Hutterite preacher and his council and, to a limited extent, John Noyes and Oneida's Central Members performed this function. In the Family, however, this element was missing. Ultimate decisions came from its charismatic leader, Lord Byron, and not through an autocratic hierarchy. Continuity and stability were in constant jeopardy.

In Oneida John Noyes had created an autocratic structure, but, like the Family, it did not continue to exist for long. Noyes as leader either made all the major decisions or could veto those not originating with him. As a charismatic figure he was successful in isolating himself from the members and managed to maintain a certain mystery and awe. He refused to relinquish his complete dictatorial powers. Unlike the Hutterites, the Oneida member had no feeling of participation in decisions affecting the commune.

Only in Hutterite social and cultural organization is there a structured hierarchy allowing for a diffusion of power in clearly defined roles for all persons through all levels of the community. Wisely, authority is not completely left to the charismatic leader. There is a feeling here among all members, especially in the church, where major decisions are made, that they function not outside of the hierarchy (the order of God), but within it. As long as these conditions are maintained the Hutterites will likely survive. The inability of the Family and of Oneida to make transitions from the charismatic-led commune to the structured autocratic form was a major factor in their discontinuity.

There are those in modern communes who believe that it is possible to go from charismatic authority to a community with no structured authority (anarchy) or to a community without either personal charisma or defined structure. Anthropology will be alert to any such developments.

6

The Modern
Communal Movement

The many communes and communal living arrangements that have come into existence in recent years reflect new awarenesses that have been developing in modern society. The word commune may not be the most appropriate term for many of these new associations, however, for some are typically domestic units (i.e., homes, as opposed to communal villages or towns) averaging perhaps a dozen adults plus attendant children. The various philosophic origins are reflected in correspondingly diverse life styles. Many are attempts to establish new and more enduring interpersonal relationships. Some are doubtless rooted in negative responses to the established institutions of society and to specific grievances such as the collapse of the civil rights movement, the escalation of the war in Indo-China, and the feeling of helplessness in a world caught up in bureaucracy.

The interest in communes and in what has been called "alternate culture" has been so widespread and so seriously motivated that it cannot be dismissed as a mere passing fad. A growing body of literature is evident in the flood of books and articles on communes. Filling the need for communication and information have been several hundred underground newspapers supported by underground wire services. Scores of journals exist, covering a wide range of issues from the most technical to the most esoteric. There are switchboard connections in every major city to alternate culture groups. As part of the dissemination process religious organizations, some with many chapters, are evangelizing for Hindu or Buddhist sects in the United States. One of the more well-known movements, the Jesus movement has seen a period of great expansion. Underground churches and house churches have emerged from the sects within the three major denominations. The Bahai, Quaker, and Unitarian fellowships have formed communitarian experiments of several kinds. Hundreds of human growth centers have sprung up, to mention nothing of the free-school movement that has gained considerable momentum simultaneously with the commune movement.

Hardly a small undertaking, such activities have necessitated ingenious methods of raising capital. Graphic art, poetry, and theater groups, as well as craftsmanship —the making of pottery, leather goods, candles, and jewelry—have supported the activities of alternate culture groups. Musical and artistic enrichment has resulted, and new art forms have been created. Live and recorded folk, rock, and modern ballads have been nourished in alternate culture groups. Cookbooks and recipes utilizing wild plants and ancient customs have enlarged the scope of traditional nutrition concepts. Of the many new catalogs, *The Whole Earth Catalog* is the most famed for providing ideas, contacts, and resources in depth.

The disenchantment with mainstream, modern affluent culture is one of the remarkable features of the "youth culture" in American society. Their rebellion may be regarded as normal in most societies, but what was unique in the sixties was the fact that large numbers of white young people, mostly apolitical, were alienated from their economically, educationally, and socially privileged families. There is a certain element of madness in the counterculture, and for these persons, this necessary differentiation, either by going mad or by developing new forms of consciousness, represents a form of inner growth. Critics of society have articulated their dissatisfactions: Not only have writers elucidated the nature of interpersonal degeneration and alienation in the midst of abundance, but behavioral scientists talk about the scarcity of rituals and meaningful symbols in mainstream culture. Disillusioned youth have rejected the dream of convenience, wherein each nuclear family has a private home within easy reach of a metropolitan center, with air-conditioning, central heating, a complex of appliances, several automobiles, telephones, television sets, free (compulsory) schooling through the bachelor's degree, adequate police and fire protection, insurance for life and property—the list is endless. Middle-class houses and their living rooms, they say, are funeral parlors.

To the anthropologist the rise of the commune movement cannot be attributed only to hippies and to the young reacting against the materialistic culture of their parents. From this perspective the movement is not an aberration at all, but a logical step in the progression of human culture. The movement may represent a single generation's response to deficiencies in parental culture, to neglect of their personal needs. Young people in the sixties were forced to develop a "new" culture because there was no real culture in which they could participate. Though parents believed their family life was normal or "ideal" as Americans understood it, they were actually raising their children for a world that was unattainable or which had room for only a limited few. Perhaps the pressure for upward mobility was so great that upon reaching adulthood they found themselves unable to participate in the roles of society. The creation of new roles in the form of communes was a cultural necessity, serving an important societal function, and they may be here to stay. Members enter the commune upon reaching young adulthood and leave it after passing through a period of self-discovery, having acquired some competence in relating to adult roles. Arranged around peer group relations, such communes have little or no provision for either rearing children or transmitting the culture beyond tomorrow.

The attrition rate of communes is high, and many collapse while others are being formed. Specific communes fail, but the idea of communal living seems to be thriving. Persons who persist in making communal living their way of life struggle through many experiments to discover what works for them. A successful youth commune, therefore, cannot be measured by longevity but by the personal rewards it brings to the individual participant and the larger societal functions it serves.

Much discussion has ensued from the communitarian controversy, and many questions have been posed. What is the future of the communitarian movement? What effect will it have upon society in general? Do communes have to operate as closed systems in order to be successful? What is the role of women *vis-à-vis* males in communitarian movements? Why is a structured communitarian group more likely to survive than one that has very little autocracy? Such questions deserve further study, but to date there are only partial answers.

Enduring communal societies like the agricultural collectives in Russia and China, kibbutzim in Israel, the Hutterites, and village communes have firm social structures based on explicit beliefs, rules, patterns of governance, and customs, visible as a skeleton. The newer communes, however, have an invisible structure, more like that of a skeleton hidden beneath the flesh, a metaphor suggested by Judson Jerome (1974). The social structure is not obvious, and although it can be intuited and hypothesized by the observer, it remains implicit—so much so that the members in a youth commune themselves are often unaware that it exists. While this type has been described by some as anarchistic, it may be more correct to say that such communes prefer to function by unstated rather than stated laws. They are retreats seeking Eden rather than Utopia, spontaneity and natural order rather than imposed social order.

Rosabeth Kanter (1972:174–212) categorizes two forms of association as "retreat" communes and "communes with missions." Retreat communes tend to be small, anarchistic, easily dissolved, predominantly rural and youth-oriented, and having boundaries that are largely negative and based on protest. They are born of rebellion and seek to escape the ills of society. In urban areas they generally limit their goals to forming new social relationships rather than forming new communities. "Communes with missions" are distinguished by having a committed core group interacting with the larger society through service. "Their mission gives them the focus around which to erect affirmative boundaries." Koinonia Farm in Americus, Georgia, for example, is concerned with the affirmation of Christian community living expressed in assisting the rural poor and with ending segregation. Synanon is a therapeutic community concerned with the rehabilitation of drug addicts. Thus while retreat communes seek withdrawal from mainstream society, service communes seek involvement and sometimes define their goal as "helpers" or reformers.

Some communes have taken the position, as did the Family, that they are forming a new culture. Their basic premise is that by concerted will they can divorce themselves from the parent culture and design a society in which they can be "more free." The anthropologist looks at such an undertaking and asks "Just how free?" He wants to know which social forms are a survival of the parent cultures; what the minimal requisites are for the formation of a culture; what can, in fact, be altered by concerted group action. That large groups of people can understand society well enough to suddenly abandon their cultural forms and invent new ones by sheer will or intention appears unlikely. Communards generally are involved in their subject, and it is rare that a participant can at the same time have the objectivity to write a successful ethnography of his own commune.

Students in anthropology must develop guidelines for understanding the body of literature on the communal movement. When reading a report of a communal group, it is helpful to ascertain where the writer stands in relationship to the group he is observing. Even the very best ethnography is likely to be colored by personal biases. If the writer has made clear his personal stake in the society, it becomes easier to read his work objectively.

Statistically speaking, there are few people living in intentional communes—perhaps not enough to warrant the attention given to the phenomenon by the press. Judson Jerome states in his forthcoming book *Families of Eden*, that by considerable "guessing and extrapolation" he has been able to estimate that three out of a thousand persons in the United States population are living communally. (By comparison, the entire kibbutz population constitutes about 4 percent of the Israeli population.) The interest of large numbers of young men and women in communal living, together with an active inquisitive press, seems to have anticipated that experimental communities would yield some important message for the larger society.

Although this "message" is diverse, representing innumerable points of view, there are some discernible ideals among the pioneering communards:

1. *Real needs must be distinguished from pecuniary needs.* Communes reject the dehumanizing, standardized apartment, the multi-garaged, gadget-filled suburban mansion, and the incessant acquisition of objects. Living in "a society filled with gadgets and junk and Madison Avenue ad men" (Fairfield 1972:361) has made man too dependent on material things.
2. *Alienated man must return to a natural, human habitat.* Human beings must find ways to get away from the pollution, congestion, freeways, and foul odors of the cities. Ecological awareness, living with nature, feeling soil rather than concrete, breathing clean air, learning to plant grass and trees are dignities of which man has been deprived.
3. *Human relationships must be restructured in such a way as to allow for sharing of the whole person, not only intelligence, but also body and spirit.* A generation of isolated, lonely, competitive people, trapped by the nuclear family and television, is deprived of the basic knowledge of how to be human and, how to live in natural family relationships. The old extended family, related by blood and marriage ties, must be replicated in new forms where people come together to re-establish relationships that allow for human sharing. The commune is the logical place for regeneration and self-knowledge.
4. *Communes provide a means for self-discovery and exposure to a broader range of human potential.* Mainstream culture places a lopsided emphasis on getting a college degree and a good job, getting married, and raising a family. Over-balanced stresses limit the development of the whole person. Putting arms around one another while chanting and swaying dramatizes how communal people try to rid themselves of anything that separates one individual from another.
5. *The criteria of successful communal living is not the longevity of a commune.* Individual fulfillment is a more appropriate measure of success. After all, many of the so-called "successful" communes (Shakers, Ephrata, Harmony Society) repressed creativity, individuality, intellectual activity, and even sexuality. Finally, it must be noted that among the most "successful" institutions for maintaining continuity are prisons.

References

Carden, Maren Lockwood, 1969, *Oneida: Utopian Community to Modern Corporation*. Baltimore: Johns Hopkins Press.

Eaton, J. W., and A. J. Mayer, 1954, *Man's Capacity to Reproduce: The Demography of a Unique Population*. New York: Free Press.

Fairfield, Richard, 1972, *Communes U.S.A., A Personal Tour*. Baltimore: Penguin Books.

Hall, Edward T., 1959, *The Silent Language*. Garden City, N.Y.: Doubleday & Company.

Holloway, Mark, 1951, *Heavens on Earth: Utopian Communities in America, 1680–1880*. London: Turnstile Press. New York: Dover Press edition, 1966.

Horowitz, David, Michael P. Lerner, and Craig Pyres, 1972, *Counterculture and Revolution*. New York: Random House.

Hostetler, John A., and Gertrude E. Huntington, 1967, *The Hutterites in North America*. New York: Holt, Rinehart and Winston, Inc.

Howlett, Duncan, 1957, *The Essenes and Christianity*. New York: Harper & Row.

Jerome, Judson, 1974, *Families of Eden: Communes and the New Anarchism*. New York: Seabury Press.

Kanter, Rosabeth, 1972, *Commitment and Community: Communes and Utopia in Sociological Perspective*. Cambridge, Mass.: Harvard University Press.

Kateb, George, 1968, "Utopia," in *International Encyclopedia of the Social Sciences*, Vol. 16. New York: Macmillan Company.

Kroeber, A. L., 1952, *The Nature of Culture*. Chicago: University of Chicago Press.

Littell, Franklin H., 1965, "Prefatory Essay," in *The Communistic Societies of the United States*, by Charles Nordhoff. New York: Schocken Books.

Lockwood, Maren, 1965, "The Experimental Utopia in America," in *Utopian and Utopian Thought*, ed. Frank E. Manuel. Boston: Beacon Press.

Nordhoff, Charles, original edition 1875, *The Communistic Societies of the United States*. New York: Hillary House, 1960; New York: Schocken Books, 1965.

Parker, Robert Allerton, 1935, *A Yankee Saint, John Humphrey Noyes and the Oneida Community*. New York: G. P. Putnam's Sons.

Plath, David, ed., 1971, *Aware of Utopia*. Urbana, Ill.: University of Illinois Press.

Robertson, Constance Noyes, ed., 1970, *Oneida Community: An Autobiography, 1851–1876*. Syracuse, N.Y.: Syracuse University Press.

————, 1972, *Oneida Community: The Breakup, 1876–1881*. Syracuse, N.Y.: Syracuse University Press.

Roszak, Theodore, 1969, *The Making of a Counterculture*. Garden City, N.Y.: Doubleday & Company.

Troeltsch, Ernst, 1931, *The Social Teachings of the Christian Churches*, trans. by O. Wyon. New York: Macmillan. Later edition in 2 vols.: New York: Free Press, 1949.

Tyler, Alice F., 1944, *Freedom's Ferment*. Minneapolis: University of Minnesota Press.

Westues, Kenneth, 1972, *Society's Shadow: Studies in the Sociology of Countercultures*. Toronto, Canada: Ryerson Press.

Selected Readings

GENERAL INTRODUCTION TO
THE MODERN COMMUNAL MOVEMENT

Fairfield, Richard, 1972, *Communes U.S.A., A Personal Tour*. Baltimore: Penguin Books.

Hedgepeth, William, and Dennis Stock, 1971, *The Alternative*. New York: Macmillan.

Jerome, Judson, 1974, *Families of Eden: Communes and the New Anarchism*. New York: Seabury Press.

Melville, Keith, 1972, *Communes in the Counter Culture: Origins, Theories, Styles of Life*. New York: William Morrow and Company.

Roberts, Ron, 1971, *The New Communes*. Englewood Cliffs, N.J.: Prentice-Hall, Inc.

Teselle, Sally, 1973, *Family Communes and Utopian Societies*. New York: Harper & Row.

DESCRIPTIVE STUDIES OF COMMUNITARIAN SOCIETIES

Amana

Shambaugh, B. M., 1932, *Amana That Was and Amana That Is*. Iowa City, Iowa: State Historical Society of Iowa.

American Indian

Dozier, Edward P., 1966, *Hano: A Tewa Indian Community in Arizona*. New York: Holt, Rinehart and Winston, Inc.

Amish

Hostetler, J. A., 1968, *Amish Society*. Baltimore: Johns Hopkins Press.

Hostetler, J. A., and G. E. Huntington, *Children in Amish Society*. New York: Holt, Rinehart and Winston, Inc.

Doukhobor

Hawthorne, Harry B., ed., 1955, *The Doukhobors of British Columbia*.

Woodcock, George, and Ivan Avakumovic, 1968, *The Doukhobors*. Toronto, Canada and New York: Oxford University Press.

Ephrata

Ernst, James E., 1963, *Ephrata: A History*. Allentown, Pa.: Schlechters.

Hippie

Partridge, William L., 1973, *The Hippie Ghetto*. New York: Holt, Rinehart and Winston, Inc.

Hutterite

Bennett, John, 1967, *Hutterian Brethren*. Stanford, California: Stanford University Press.

Hostetler, J. A., and G. E. Huntington, 1967, *The Hutterites in North America*. New York: Holt, Rinehart and Winston, Inc.

Japanese

Sugihara, Yoshie, and David Plath, 1969, *Sensei and His People: The Story of the Building of a Japanese Commune.* Berkeley, Calif.: University of California Press.

Jewish, Eastern Europe

Zborowski, Mark, and Elizabeth Herzof, 1952, *Life Is with People, The Culture of the Shtetl.* New York: Schocken Books.

Kibbutz

Spiro, Melford E., 1956, *Kibbutz: Venture in Utopia.* Cambridge, Mass.: Harvard University Press.

Mennonite, Old Colony

Redekop, Calvin W., 1969, *The Old Colony Mennonites: Dilemmas of Ethnic Minority Life.* Baltimore: Johns Hopkins Press.

Oneida

Carden, Maren Lockwood, 1969, *Oneida, Utopian Community to Modern Corporation.* Baltimore: Johns Hopkins Press.
Robertson, Constance Noyes, ed., 1970, *Oneida Community: An Autobiography, 1851–1876.* Syracuse, N.Y.: Syracuse University Press.

Shaker

Andrews, Edward D., 1963, *The People Called Shakers.* New York: Dover Publications.

Society of Brothers

Zablocki, Benjamin D., 1971, *The Joyful Community.* Baltimore: Penguin Books.

Synanon

Yablonsky, Lewis, 1967, *Synanon: The Tunnel Back.* Baltimore: Penguin Books.

UTOPIANISM AND HISTORICAL COMMUNES

Bestor, A. E., Jr., 1950, *Backwoods Utopias, 1663–1829.* Philadelphia: University of Pennsylvania Press.
Buber, Martin, 1949, *Paths to Utopia,* New York: Macmillan Company.
Cohen, Norman, 1961, *The Pursuit of the Millennium.* New York: Oxford University Press. Revised edition.
Holloway, Mark, 1951, *Heavens on Earth: Utopian Communities in America, 1680–1880.* London: Turnstile Press.
Howlett, Duncan, 1957, *The Essenes and Christianity.* New York: Harper & Row.
Kanter, Rosabeth, 1972, *Commitment and Community: Communes and Utopia in Sociological Perspective.* Cambridge, Mass.: Harvard University Press.
Kateb, George, 1963, *Utopia and Its Enemies.* New York: Free Press.
Kautsky, Karl, 1966, *Communism in Central Europe in the Time of the Reformation,* trans. by J. L. and E. G. Mullikin. London: Reprint of 1899 edition.

Mannheim, Karl, 1936, *Ideology and Utopia: An Introduction to the Sociology of Knowledge.* New York: Harcourt Brace Jovanovich, Inc.

Manuel, Frank E., ed., 1967, *Utopia and Utopian Thought.* Boston: Beacon Press.

Mumford, Lewis, 1923, *The Story of Utopias: Ideal Commonwealths and Social Myths.* New York: Gaer Associates.

Nordhoff, Charles, original edition 1875, *The Communistic Societies of the United States.* New York: Schocken Books, 1965.

Plath, David W., ed., 1971, *Aware of Utopia.* Urbana, Ill.: University of Illinois Press.

Skinner, B. F., 1948, *Walden Two.* New York: Macmillan Company.

Tyler, Alice F., 1944, *Freedom's Ferment.* Minneapolis: University of Minnesota Press, Harper Torchbook edition, 1962. *See* Part Two, "Cults and Utopias."

Webber, Everett, 1959, *Escape to Utopia: The Communal Movement in America.* New York: Hastings House.

Westhues, Kenneth, 1972, *Society's Shadow: Studies in the Sociology of Counter-cultures.* Toronto, Canada: Ryerson Press.

Questions

1. Define utopian. In what sense are all societies utopian?

2. What distinguishes a counterculture group from a communitarian group?

3. What beliefs (ideology) did the three communitarian groups profess that were not put into actual practice? Make a list of several in each of the three groups.

4. What discrepancies existed between belief and practice in the Family? In Oneida? In the Hutterite group?

5. Compare the ethnocentric pattern of the three communitarian groups.

6. What beliefs regulated the use of resources in the three groups?

7. Describe the social stratification (or classification) of members in the Hutterite society. Compare this with the Family and with Oneida.

8. Which of the three groups would be least likely to accept a total stranger as a member of their group? Why?

9. Describe the role of the mother in the Hutterite group. Compare this role with Oneida and the Family.

10. Which of the three groups had the greatest institutional provision for the care of children? Which had the least?

11. In which of the three groups can the nuclear family function best without the threat of disrupting the social system? Why?

12. How are rules made in the Family? In Oneida? In Hutterite society? In which of the three does consensus play an important part in decision making?

Case Study
Interactions*

1. Read William L. Partridge, *The Hippie Ghetto* (1973), and compare this cultural system with that of the Family on the following characteristics: ideology, economy, social patterns, and internal authority.
2. Edward P. Dozier, in his Case Study, *Hano: A Tewa Indian Community in Arizona* (1966), discusses a kind of communitarian society that has survived on the North American continent for centuries. Compare the beliefs of the Pueblos to those of the Family, Oneida, and the Hutterites. Can you rank the four cultural systems from most to least ethnocentric?
3. Both the Amish and the Hutterites are surviving Anabaptist communal societies who have many similar professed religious beliefs. Compare the goals of socialization in these two societies using J. A. Hostetler and G. E. Huntington, *The Hutterites in North America* (1967) and, by the same authors, *Children in Amish Society* (1971). What are the major differences in goals? In which society does the individual have greater personal control over his behavior? In which society is formal schooling given greater emphasis? Why? In which does the nuclear family perform a greater function in the socialization process?
4. Read Jerry Jacobs's *Fun City: An Ethnographic Study of a Retirement Community* (1974), a description of a white, American, middle-class retirement community in California. What are the most contrastive differences between this community and the Family, Oneida, and the Hutterites? Can you see ways in which the communitarian movement could be a reaction to some aspects of the way of life reported for Fun City? Which aspects?
5. William Pilcher in *The Portland Longshoremen: A Dispersed Urban Community* (1972) reports upon a male-oriented, blue-collar group that has roots deep in midwestern rural America. This group rejects the concept of social mobility as intrinsically worthless; any display of superior social status is repugnant. In the behavior and values of this group do you see any parallels to those of any of the communities reported in this Basic Unit? How do the longshoremen go about solving some of the same problems of survival, group relations, communication, family life, social control, and so on, that are faced by the communitarian groups?

* See Relevant Case Studies listed on page 64.

Relevant Case Studies*

Buechler, Hans, and Judith-Maria Buechler, 1970, *The Bolivian Aymara*. This Case Study focuses on Compi, a community on the shores of Lake Titicaca on the Bolivian High Plateau. Compi is viewed as a part of a wider social, temporal, and spatial framework. The economic organization and its changes, as well as the fiesta system and a system of sponsorship called Cargo, which is widespread in Latin America, are covered. The latter system in particular makes an interesting contrast to the communitarian ideal.

Dozier, Edward P., 1966, *Hano: A Tewa Indian Community in Arizona*. Hano is an American Indian community very similar to that of other western Pueblo peoples like the Hopi and the Zuni. In many ways the Tewa community at Hano seems to represent the ideal of some communitarian movements, and yet there are very important differences. The passage of time is marked by many rituals and ceremonies. The way of life is highly organized and restrained, and their socioreligious system is theocratic.

Friedl, Ernestine, 1962, *Vasilika: A Village in Modern Greece*. This Case Study shows the interrelation among such things as land resources, cotton cultivation, division of labor, concepts of cleanliness and order, the furnishing of homes, the dowry system, and ceremonies and festivities so that an integrated, patterned way of life emerges. The reader acquires insight into the quality of interpersonal relationships in Vasilika, which, like those between man and nature, are characterized by constant struggle. This focus provides a good point for comparative analysis.

Halpern, Joel, and Barbara Halpern, 1972, *A Serbian Village in Cultural Perspective*. This Case Study provides historical perspective for the community called Orasac and yet deals with changes concomitant with modernization. It places Orasac in the context of the larger national whole. Special attention is given to the *Zadruga*, a basic familial social unit in Serbian peasant life that provides interesting comparisons to communes such as the Family.

Hostetler, John A., and Gertrude E. Huntington, 1967, *The Hutterites in North America*. The Hutterites, described briefly in this Basic Unit, have formed a most significant communitarian society. This Case Study stresses the Hutterite world view and the child training and education that make a Hutterite.

Hostetler, John A., and Gertrude E. Huntington, 1971, *Children in Amish Society: Socialization and Community Education*. Amish schooling maintains the Amish culture and identity under severe social and political pressure. This Case Study in Education and Culture, together with the Hutterite Case Study by the same authors, provides a basis for understanding the crucial role of education in cultural maintenance and raises significant questions about this function in other communitarian societies.

Jacobs, Jerry, 1974, *Fun City: An Ethnographic Study of a Retirement Community*. A study of an activity-centered, as well as age-centered, planned retirement community in a warm valley of the West. Despite its 92 clubs and organizations, however, most of its 5600 inhabitants do not lead what could be described as an active life, and the community as a whole is marked by a low degree of integration.

* Edited by George and Louise Spindler, and published by Holt, Rinehart and Winston, Inc. as Case Studies in Cultural Anthropology and Case Studies in Education and Culture.

Partridge, William L., 1973, *The Hippie Ghetto: The Natural History of a Subculture.* A former participant and observer of a hippie ghetto in Florida describes the social organization, activities, values, and sentiments of its inhabitants. Themes are the relation of the hippie community to mainstream culture and the hippie culture as a social movement. While the communitarian orientation of this group is convergent in some respects with those described in this Basic Unit, it is widely divergent in others.

Pilcher, William, 1972, *The Portland Longshoremen: A Dispersed Urban Community.* This blue-collar group provides sharp contrasts with the communitarian societies described in this Basic Unit. Yet in certain areas, such as the union and the behavior of its members, the longshoremen appear highly cooperative, even communitarian in a sense.

ALSO OF INTEREST

Otterbein, Keith F., 1972, *Comparative Cultural Analysis: An Introduction to Anthropology.* This textbook is specifically directed at comparison between cultures and can be used as a basis for the comparisons suggested under the Projects section of this Basic Unit. Contrastive procedures are developed throughout the text with examples drawn from *The Semai* by Robert Dentan and *Yąnomamö* by Napoleon Chagnon. The important topics and key concepts of cultural anthropology are laid out systematically, and a comparative data sheet listing 32 questions is included.